I0421602

Aleksandar DONSKI

THE ANTI-USA PROPAGANDA EXPOSED!

HOW THE ANTI-USA PROPAGANDA ACTS, AND HOW TO DEAL WITH IT

Translation:
Lubomir Donski

Lecture:
Mario Hristovski
Nikola Mitevski

ISBN-13:
978-1515330578

ISBN-10:
1515330575

2015

Aleksandar DONSKI

THE ANTI-USA PROPAGANDA EXPOSED!
HOW THE ANTI-USA PROPAGANDA ACTS, AND HOW TO DEAL WITH IT

TABLE OF CONTENTS

1. INTRODUCTION

Nowadays, it seems that is in fashion all around the world to criticize and attack the USA in every possible opportunity anytime and anywhere. This trend seems parallel with the growth and power of the USA itself. The more powerful USA is, the bigger the negative critics are. Should Americans be concerned about this? The answer is well, both yes and no. The propaganda against the USA that is present in many countries (whether it is an official government policy or a policy of a group of individuals or non-government organizations) is a confirmation of the USA status as the most powerful country in the world. And it is well known that only the most capable can reach the top. In other words, it is a kind of an "unwritten rule" to attack or be against those who are on the top, not only in politics, but in many other areas as well (music, movies, sport etc.). From this point of view, Americans should be "proud" of the fact that their country is the most criticized country in the world, because it is an indirect proof for their capability as a nation.

On the other hand, leading an unscrupulous propaganda against the USA has also a negative side, which should not be underestimated. This campaign can evoke various negative consequences. Some of them are:

a) Installation of expressive anti-USA oriented regimes in some countries. The procedure of installing such regimes is quite simple and it follows the same formula of organized groups starting to spread well-organized and aggressive anti-USA propaganda, accusing the Americans for all the evilness in their country or anywhere in the world. Usually these accusations are rarely opposed, so a large part of the citizens of that country began to believe that they are "real". As a result, these citizens begin to accept an anti-

USA mood and after some time they begin to vote for anti-USA political options. These political options, after coming to power, put their anti-USA orientation as one of the main priorities in their foreign policy. This way at the worlds' political stage another state (regime) appears that supports animosity against the USA. In worst case scenario, if this happens in several countries, it can provoke new complications at the worlds' political stage, such as forming of the new alliances as well anti-USA based pacts.

b) The lack of safety of the ordinary American citizens while traveling abroad. It is obvious that this is closely connected with the results of the anti-USA propaganda. This lack of safety is mostly expressed in two forms:

The first one is a suspicion against the Americans among citizens living in a country where the anti-USA propaganda acts. This way, good-willed American tourists, even the humanitarian workers that eventually visited to help the particular country, are labeled as "CIA spies", "intelligence agents" etc. These occasions are most common among individuals or organized subjects in the post-communist countries, where decades of paranoia was systematically raised in the conscience of the citizens (this topic will be further explained). But such occasions can be also found in other countries (European democracies, countries in which Islam is dominant).

The second form is far more dangerous and serious and it is refer to physically attacks, threats, kidnappings or even killings of the innocent people just because they are Americans. This form is most common in the countries in which Islam is dominant, but can be found in other countries as well.

c) Economic consequences. These consequences are based on the negative approach towards American products by individuals or organized groups influenced by the anti-USA propaganda. The most famous Americans products are verbally attacked and boycotted. Synonym for this perhaps is Coca-Cola which is often labeled as a "bad kind of drug" as a "dirty water of the capitalism" etc.

d) Cultural consequences. These consequences are based on the negative approach on American cultural values by individuals or organized subjects influenced by the anti-USA propaganda. Usually these attacks are against rock-music, American movies, and even American writers, or any kind of artists. I am not saying that some of these movies or other forms of art should not be criticized, but some subjects are attacking any form of art whether it is good or bad, because of one simple reason – they are American!

The economic and cultural consequences from the anti-USA propaganda are not the only negative consequences from this propaganda. Actually, a few years ago the State Department issued a public statement regarding these negative effects and the fall of the USA reputation in the world. It was also announced that certain actions will be taken in improving this condition.

Prior to presenting the main part of my research, I would like to point out a few more important things that should be considered:

1. I undertook the research on the anti-USA propaganda not only within particular mediums in my homeland, the Republic of Macedonia, but in a wider area as well (having on mind the fact that with internet, a large variety of mediums from all around the world are available to contact). I would like to point out that my country has a friendly orientation towards the USA. The main political parties in Macedonia have a policy of alliance and cooperation with the USA. Macedonia is also participating in every peace campaign lead by the USA. Among the largest part of the Macedonians there is

no an anti-American mood unlike in some other countries. In fact the Americans (as well other foreigners) are treated very well and warm with the traditional Macedonian hospitality and this can be confirmed by many Americans or any foreigners that have visited Macedonia. This means that the anti-USA propaganda in my country is present only within isolated cases and its' exponents are individuals or marginal organized, although most of them are well- established in some mediums or the internet.

2. Some may notice that the analysis based on the mediums I have consulted is not a complete reflection of the anti-USA propaganda across the world because only a limited amount of mediums are involved. My answer to this is that the anti-USA propaganda is essentially led by the same principles all over the world. For example, if the anti-Americans claim that the virus of AIDS is "created by the USA to get rid of black people" and if this false claim and canard expands, it would not matter if I have read it in some European, Asian, Latin-American or African medium. The content would be the same.

I will not necessary always mention names of mediums, journalists or analytics in order not to be understood that this are against someone personally. Ultimately, names do not matter. What matters is the content of the anti-USA acts and deeds, the ways this propaganda is led and the possible options for its prevention.

3. The researching of the anti-USA propaganda is made by my own initiative. I have always felt pro-Western mostly because of the freedom and democracy in the Western countries, unlike the non-freedom and restrictions that existed in the communist countries, as was Republic of Macedonia when it was a part of Yugoslavia.

I come from an artistic family. Both my parents

were painters, and my father, who loved classical art, was also a writer. Growing up, my family, although average Macedonians and not members of the Communist party, believed in the communist propaganda and in communism as an ideology that brings "equality to all", that will "end the labor exploitation" and will bring "happiness to everybody". But at the same time, my parents were orthodox Christians which was contrary to the communist ideology, something I have always noted. On one hand, my parents were admirers of the communist ideology, but on the other hand, we were secretly celebrating all Christian feasts. To make things clear, religion was not banned in communist Yugoslavia but if one were to declare as being religious, the chances of finding a job and advancing in career were decreased since these people were regarded as being suspicious and ineligible by the leading communist party activists. Furthermore, schools had lectures on Marxism and the regime-controlled mediums were spreading anti-religious propaganda based on the Karl Marx's contention that "the religion is opium of the people". This resulted in frustration among the kids raised in religious families – a feeling that if you celebrate your Christian feasts, you are a wrongdoer in the eyes of the majority. One day while I was still a boy, I watched a TV-show about American hippies and I saw that a few hippies had a cross sign on their necklaces. I was confused at first, but then filled with inner admiration. It cheered me up to know that at least someone in the world is celebrating religion without hiding. Also, I have realized that if hippies can publicly celebrate a religion, then USA must be a place where freedom of choice is respected – something that we did not have. This is the way my thoughts developed in the years that followed. Then came the western rock music, which was also a form and expression of a personal freedom that slowly took over Yugoslavia, and it definitely fixed my conviction that the personal freedom

9

does exist in the western countries. And it is something I have encountered for the first time from the Americans.

Today I still have respect for the USA for being a leader of the free world. Americans should be proud of the fact that their country is the most powerful and one of the richest in the world. I, as a Macedonian, can understand this to a certain point, since centuries ago in the time of Alexander the Great, my country Macedonia was a superpower as well, which conquered the Greeks, the Persians and any other nations that military opposed it. On the other hand, Alexander gave huge privileges to the countries that welcomed him in a friendly way. Macedonians were also a subject of a negative propaganda at that time because of their power (same as today's USA), and only a few nations can brag about being the most powerful countries in the world. Macedonia once had this status, but today it is the USA and as it seems, they will stay on the top for a very long time.

4. The content of this text should not be considered or understood as an attempt for amnesty of the false moves and deeds that the USA governments undertook in their internal and foreign policies in the past – the moves that deserve criticism. In other words, my attention is towards the indelicate attacks against the USA, which are characterized with an extremely one-sided presentation of some situations or with presenting a completely false image of the real picture and sometimes even creating insolent lies (which we will examine further). I have nothing against argumentative criticism towards the USA - what bothers me are the fake and dishonest imputations and propaganda against this country.

5. I would like to say something about the way Americans abroad react after mentioning the topic about the anti-USA propaganda (at least according to my personal experience). From my personal contacts with

10

Americans, both in and out of my country, I can say that they all reacted almost identically. At first sight, when they were told about anti-USA propaganda being spread through the mediums, they seem bit confused, and after that, they start to treat this question as a taboo topic. I have also realized that the Americans are quite engaged in the problems within their country, as well other countries. They are usually divided into liberals and conservatives (Democrats and Republicans), fiercely debating each other about the problems in their own country. They also show interest about the situation in other countries as well, trying to help and to suggest solutions for the current political problems. But when asked about the anti-USA propaganda, they suddenly become silent! During one occasion in my hometown Shtip, I asked a representative from the US embassy about his opinion on the anti-USA propaganda led by the mediums and even suggested an official discussion to be organized on that matter. He acted the same way as all the previous Americans I have encountered – little confused at first, then silent for a while, then agreed upon organizing an official discussion ("*why not?*") which, of course, never happened.

What I have concluded is that the Americans in foreign countries are not at all prepared to face the anti-USA propaganda. They avoid this topic, unlike any other topic that they would gladly give their opinions (topics regarding problems in the US society, current political affairs etc.).The topic about the anti-USA propaganda is like taboo to them, so I hope this little book will help them increase the gumption in such situations.

Now let's begin to examine the main aspects of the anti-USA propaganda.

2. REASONS FOR LEADING THE ANTI-USA PROPAGANDA

According to my perception, the reasons for leading the anti-USA propaganda are usually connected with:

1. Certain actions, acts and deeds of the American foreign policy;
2. Using (abusing) the USA superiority in science;
3. Personal and group factors connected with the propagandists (offended personal and group material interest of the propagandists, frustrations, envy, jealousy etc.).

These factors can also be connected between themselves. For example, because of the fact that the USA (together with other democratic countries) assisted the fall of the communist regimes, it is understandable why the now powerless communists (after losing their material privileges) are the leaders of the anti-USA propaganda in the post-communist countries.

We will make a detailed examination of each of these reasons.

2.1 Certain actions, acts and deeds of the American foreign policy as a reason for the anti-USA propaganda

The USA administration has made actions in the past and present that are not supported by some other countries, organized subjects or individuals. There are known cases in the USA itself, where a larger part of the public and politicians admit the mistakes that their government made in the past. The most drastic example is perhaps the Vietnamese War. There is almost a consensus in the world that this war was a mistake, and this opinion is shared by a large part of the Americans too.

A second example is the atomic bombs in Japan, which are also considered to be a wrong act by the significant part of the world (including the USA) since many innocents have lost their lives.

A third example is the military interventions in Afghanistan, Serbia, Iraq and other countries, as well the open support of some dictatorships in the past and other similar actions.

All of these (today widely treated as) "mistakes" of the American foreign policy are actively and widely used as anti-USA propaganda.

However, some may notice that this is not a case of propaganda, but of an argumentative and justified criticism. For example, the Vietnamese War really happened and hundreds of thousands people really lost their lives. Can we talk about "propaganda" for an event that really happened? Is there a clear border between propaganda and a justified criticism? Let's take a look at the facts. We will keep onto a few examples that nowadays are the most exposed.

2.1.1. The Vietnamese War

Let's start with the Vietnamese War as an example of spreading an anti-USA propaganda. There are countless mediums in the world that are considering the Vietnamese War a "proof" of the continuity of the "wrong" USA foreign policy. Why is this war mentioned so often? There have been other wars in other parts of the world that were much more grimy and fierce. It is obvious that this war is used as an "argument" against every actual policy of the USA. The message behind mentioning the Vietnamese War is clear: *"If the USA made a mistake in the past (claiming that they were right*

13

all the time), then they are also making a mistake(s) in the present and will make mistakes in the future no matter what they undertake or what they say about them being right".

But, why are we claiming that the Vietnamese War (even though it really happened and deserves a justified criticism) is being used in the anti-USA propaganda around the world? The answer to this question is the facts themselves.

If you make an inquiry in different countries with the simple question "Who took part in the Vietnamese war?" I am sure that most will answer: "USA and Vietnam", i. e. "USA made war against the Vietnamese people". If you research the Vietnamese War on the internet, you will find that this statement is absolutely dominating.

However, this answer is nothing else but a typical proof of the anti-USA propaganda. Let's explain why this is so.

It is little known to the wider public that France was involved in war against Vietnam much longer than the USA. France attacked Vietnam in the mid-19th century and in the second half of the same century Vietnam was fully occupied by the French army and was turned into a French colony. In the 1880s, the Vietnamese people, led by Phan Dinh Phung, rebelled against the French colonists. Although the rebellion lasted for almost ten years, it was in the end crushed with a lot of victims. In 1930 the Vietnamese raised another rebellion against the French, but it failed too.

During the Second World War, most of Vietnam was under Japanese occupation, but after the war, the French tried to bring it back under their control. In 1945 the leader of the Vietnamese communists Ho Chi Minh proclaimed a Vietnamese state. The French replied with more military campaigns in order to take Vietnam back. In 1946, Ho Chi Minh (this time supported by the communist China) raised another rebellion against France. Fierce battles were led, but the crucial one between the Vietnamese communists and the French army at the Diem Bien Phu defeated the French. Vietnam was then separated into two parts and each proclaimed a Vietnamese state. The first one was non-democratic and communist, known as "North Vietnam", while the second one "South Vietnam" and was formally known as a democratic state, even though its regime was corrupt. Due to the danger of the communists coming into power in South Vietnam, the government of this country asked the USA for military help. This is how the USA interfered in the Vietnamese war. In fact, the whole time they were on the side of the Vietnamese democratic forces battling the Vietnamese communists. The USA intervention was from January 1965 to August 1973. In April, the northern Vietnamese communists conquered South Vietnam and to this day still rule it. This means that the war between the USA and the Vietnamese communists effectively lasted for around eight and a half years.

On the other hand, the war that France led against the Vietnamese people (with short or long intermissions), believe it or not, lasted for **eighty** years – almost ten times longer than the war led by the USA! The number of victims in these French-Vietnamese encounters is estimated to be around half a million.

But nowadays, is anyone ever talking about the French "Vietnamese war"? Is anyone today denouncing France for its military affairs against the Vietnamese people and the eight decades of military occupation? Why is the term "Vietnamese war" always associated to the American war, and not the French one which lasted almost 10 times longer? Isn't this propaganda?

But that is not all regarding the Vietnamese wars.

In February 1979 China undertook a military aggression against Vietnam. Make an inquiry on random citizens and ask them if they have ever heard about this (this time "Chinese") Vietnam War? Or is any medium today ever mentioning this war? Even though this war lasted for a month, it was quite cruel. It is estimated that during this war over sixty thousand soldiers and civilians have been killed on both sides, which means that around 200 people died daily. Why is this "Vietnamese War" also forgotten by the mediums that are dealing with the Vietnamese War? The Chinese "Vietnamese War" happened in a period closer to the present unlike the American "Vietnamese War", and yet average people rarely know about it.

There is even more regarding the Vietnamese War.

In December 1978, another "Vietnamese War" happened. This time, Vietnam itself undertook military aggression and occupied their neighboring country of Kampuchea (Cambodia), which lasted until 1989. At that time, Kampuchea was led by the horrible dictatorship of Pol Pot and his genocidal communist regime, so the Vietnamese army helped in tearing down this regime. This war was also crude with tens of thousands victims, both civilians and soldiers. So here we have another "Vietnamese War" that nowadays is barely remembered, and far away from being mentioned in the mediums.

The Vietnamese army also attacked its neighbor Laos to help the restoration of a communist regime in this country, and that regime is still ongoing to this day.

The facts are that, in the 19th and the 20th century, several Vietnamese Wars occurred. Vietnam was an aggressor and a victim of aggression, but despite the American one, none of the other wars are forced in the mediums. Isn't this a classic example of an anti-USA propaganda?

I am not claiming that the American Vietnamese War should be justified. I am just publicly asking why is the USA nowadays the only one judged for the war in Vietnam, while the other countries that also attacked

Vietnam are not even mentioned. Isn't this hypocrisy? If one feels sad for the Vietnamese for the wars they were involved in, he should also blame the other responsible countries (including Vietnam itself), not only the USA!

2.1.2. The Atomic bombs

The history of using the atomic bombs in WW2 is well known, so we will not focus on details. We will only state that even today this horrible act is also used in the anti-USA propaganda. Even though this act that ended tens of thousands civilian lives in Hiroshima and Nagasaki can never be justified, certain facts should be kept in mind. These facts nowadays are rarely mentioned or purposely "forgotten".

Namely, if the bombs were not dropped, the war would have continued for an indefinite amount of time and it is estimated that the number of victims would have been much bigger than the losses from the atomic bombs. It is known that after the dropping of the atomic bombs, some of the Japanese generals insisted on continuing the war. So it was the dropping of the bombs that convinced Japan to capitulate and put an end to World War Two.

It is a fact that the Japanese victims of the atomic bombs are much more present in the mediums unlike the victims from the Japanese genocidal aggression in parts of Eastern Asia. The USA should be criticized for dropping the atomic bombs which ended a huge number of civilian lives, but it is not right to be silent about the much bigger number of civilian victims caused by the Japanese aggressor. The Japanese militarism in World War Two was one of the most genocidal and most aggressive movements in the history of Asia. The Japanese army in China during this war killed an unbelievable number of people – somewhere between

17

20 and 37 million! For example, in 1937 in the Chinese city Nanking, the Japanese army killed around 300.000 civilians in only two months! Today horrible testimonies of the Japanese rapes and massacres are preserved. In some of these authentic testimonies (which any reader can find in relevant sources on the internet or other mediums) we read about outrageous crimes in which tens of thousands Chinese women and children were raped then killed; sons were forced to rape their mothers, fathers to rape their daughters. Even the priests in celibacy were forced to rape women. Today China is rightfully reacting against the inappropriate treatment of this outrageous massacre on civilians which is almost forgotten by the mediums worldwide. Do ordinary people from around the world know these facts? This was the same Japan that America dropped atomic bombs on, in order to end the war. Even though there is no excuse for the many lost civilian lives, the reasons as well the circumstances for dropping these atomic bombs should also be kept in mind.

The Japanese imperial army did massacre not only in China but in all the countries they have occupied during World War Two. One of them is the Philippines, where the Japanese soldiers did a massive massacre on the citizens of Manila (the capital city of Philippines). This massacre happened only a few months before the end of the war. According to the data provided from the later trials of the Japanese generals Yamashita and Muto (both sentenced to death), the Japanese soldiers killed around 100-120,000 Filipino civilians which was around 10% of the overall population of Manila. On February 13th 1945, the Japanese soldiers received a precise commandment about what to do with the dead Filipinos: *"When Filipinos are to be killed, they must be gathered into one place... Because the disposal of dead bodies is a troublesome task, they should be gathered into houses which are scheduled to be burned or demolished. They should also be thrown into the river."* (Connaughton, R., Pimlott, J., and Anderson, D., 1995, The Battle for Manila, London: Bloomsbury Publishing, ISBN 0891415785). During this massacre, massive killings were made in schools, hospitals and temples in which children and babies were brutally killed by subjects of the Japanese regular army. This was not the only massacre that the Japanese army did on the Philippines.

During the World War Two the Japanese army ordered massive massacres on civilians in Burma, which was also under their occupation. In 1942 the Japanese soldiers did a massacre in Rohingya, where thousands of men, women and children were raped, tyrannized and killed (more on this can be found at: Kurt Jonassohn, *Genocide and gross human rights violations: in comparative perspective.* 2011, p. 263.).

These massacres in Burma continued even to the very end of the war. For example, in July 7th 1945 (only around one month before the end of WW2), units from the Japanese army under the command of general Yamamato killed around six hundred civilians in the village Kalagong, under accusation for collaboration with the Brits. Again women and children were raped, and then killed. Any reader can find more information on this in relevant sources.

During World War two the Japanese had also occupied a part of Indonesia. According to the report from the UN, it is considered that around four million people died as a result of the Japanese occupation in Indonesia (Dower, John W. *War Without Mercy: Raceand Power in the Pacific War*, 1986; Pantheon).

The Japanese have also occupied Malaya and Singapore. It is estimated that in these two countries, around 25,000 to 50,000 local Chinese citizens were killed by the Japanese army.

Having these facts on mind, it becomes clearer as to why the USA decided to drop the atomic bombs on

Japan. The purpose was to put an end to the madness of the parts of the Japanese army where soldiers didn't stop massacring innocent civilians even right before the very end of the war. So when you think about the innocent Japanese victims of the atomic bombs, think also of the millions innocents that were killed by the Japanese army in several parts of Asia and are almost forgotten now.

To conclude, the aggressive Japanese militarism in World War two was the main reason for the suffering of the Japan itself, same as Hitler who was also the main reason for the destruction of Germany during the World War two.

2.1.3. The USA military interventions (Iraq, Afghanistan and others)

The USA military interventions against the regimes in Iraq and Afghanistan are used in similar connotation. Regarding this, I shall also mention some facts that should be considered. I will not talk in details about the crude regime of Saddam Hussein in Iraq or about the savage Taliban regime in Afghanistan. I will not point out the usage of chemical weapons of Saddam Hussein against the Kurds in the Iraqi part of Kurdistan in the 1980s (which was reported by the world agencies of that time) and I will also not point out the terror and occupation of Kuwait that also implemented the regime of Saddam Hussein. What I want to point out is something else.

The USA, as every other country or organized subject, even an individual, has their own interests, friends, but enemies as well. It is normal and logical the USA to act duly to their friends and enemies. This rule is followed by every country in the world – cooperation and friendship with the friendly countries, and efforts to make damage to the unfriendly countries or other kinds of organized subjects. The rule applies not only to countries, but to every other subject or individual. So, the USA relationship to the above-mentioned regimes should be viewed from this aspect. But again, the anti-USA propagandists have an incorrect attitude. Many times we have heard or read that the USA is destroying the regimes that do not fit their policy, and as examples are used the already mentioned regimes of the Taliban in Afghanistan, Saddam Hussein in Iraq, but the regime of Slobodan Milosevic in Serbia as well. Yet, the fact that these regimes were openly self-declared as enemies of the USA, i.e. the affective anti-Americanism was one of the fundaments in their foreign policies, is tendentiously avoided. This is supported by a lot of proofs. Should we be reminded that the base of Al Qaeda was hosted by the Taliban regime in Afghanistan? Should we be reminded of Saddam Hussein's regime that enacted genocide upon the Kurds and occupied the USA-friendly country Kuwait? There are also a number of proofs about the crimes of the Milosevic's regime. These crimes, together with the open anti-USA policy that this regime officially promoted (which included even calls for renewal of the Warsaw pact) were a sufficient reason for the USA to connect with the traditional enemy of Serbia – the Albanians from Kosovo, and we all know what happened next.

The biggest mistake that Milosevic made was the breakdown of the traditional Serbian-American friendship and madly putting Serbia in a conflict with the most powerful country in the world. If the pro-USA oriented Milan Panic won the presidential elections in December 1992, things would have been different. But Milosevic was chosen by the majority of the Serbian people and he led them in conflict with the most powerful countries in the world which ended catastrophically for Serbia. Unlike them, the Albanians from Kosovo played the card of friendship and cooperation with the USA and because of that they managed to fulfill their dream – Kosovo's independence. Before that (in the 1980s), the majority of Albanians from Kosovo also had a communist orientation. If we check the reports and photographs from that time when the Albanians demonstrated for Kosovo to become a republic in communists Yugoslavia, we can see that they were forcing paroles with communist content ("Marxism-Leninism" etc., which were openly anti-Western). But in the 1990s, after a favorable opportunity appeared in front of them, the Albanians from Kosovo pragmatically "forget" about the communism i.e. the anti-Americanism (unlike the majority of Serbs who supported of Milosevic) and succeeded to gain their goal.

To conclude, the USA is acting only against their enemies, but so are the rest of the countries in the world! It is quite hypocritical to judge the USA for destroying the regime of Saddam Hussein, supposedly because Hussein "did not agree with the USA's policy", while at the same time ignoring the fact that this very same dictator occupied the independent country of Kuwait. Hussein also attacked a weaker country that did not agree with his policies, so there is no reason for his supporters to get angry, since they received the same fate – his regime was attacked by a stronger country. Even more drastic is the example with the regime of Slobodan Milosevic. This regime had previously carried Serbia in war and hostility with almost every weaker neighboring country than Serbia that was part of the former Yugoslavia. Back then, not even one of his followers stated that Milosevic was attacking the weaker countries that did not agree with his policy, but when the same fate happened to them, i.e. when his regime was attacked by stronger countries - they suddenly started to complain this (which is understandable, but immoral). As for the savage regime of the Taliban, the USA practically did a favor to the whole world by destroying it. Some remains of this regime are still making crimes and massacres on the civilians not only in Afghanistan, but also in the neighboring country Pakistan. The biggest massacre happened on 16th December 2014 in the Pakistani city Peshawar, where the Taliban savages killed 130 innocent children. Knowing these facts, I wonder what kind of morality does one need to have to judge the USA for destroying the Taliban regime.

It is understandable that the reaction against one country's enemy depends on the power of that country. Let's take as an example the Palestinians and the Jews. What do you think will happen if the Palestinians had the military power of the USA? My small country Republic of Macedonia also has had a dispute with Greece for decades. The Greeks negate the national identity of the Macedonians not only in my country, but to the Macedonian minority that lives in Greece too. I wonder if Greece would act the same way, if my country had at least 10% of the military and economic power of the USA. This means that the USA is treating their enemies in accordance and proportion with their own power (military and economic) and I don't find it odd - every country in the world does the same. It is up to the less powerful countries to decide whether they will join the most powerful country in the world, or enter a reckless confrontation that will result in an obvious outcome.

At the end of this heading we will mention another accusation against the Americans and that is when some subjects are calling them "a genocidal nation", since they exterminated the indigenous people of the USA territory – the Indians. It is true that the first European settlers came into conflict with the indigenous people (in USA, they were Indians) right after their first settlement on the American continent. This battle continued even after the forming of the USA as an independent country. The Indians lost this battle on territory because of their weaker armament and lesser cultural development. It is a hard truth, but it is not connected only with the Indians. There are many examples in the history in which the more powerful nations have exterminated or evicted the less powerful indigenous ones. Sadly, this "Law of the jungle" was a part of the human life. In fact, every battle was (and still is) to gain a territory (living space). For example, I am part of the Macedonian nation. In 1913, part of my fatherland was occupied by Greece and since then hundreds of thousands Macedonians were expatriated or killed by the Greek regimes, and afterwards replaced (in the Macedonians cities and villages) by Greeks from Asia. Nowadays, as a result to this, the ethnic composition of this part of Macedonia is completely replaced. Yet, why is no one talking about this Greek genocide on the ethnic Macedonians? Such kinds of wars continued even to the end of the 20th century. Let's mention the wars in former Yugoslavia, where hundreds of thousands Bosniaks (Muslims), Serbs and Croats were killed or harassed in order to leave their homes, i.e. to recede their territory and living place to the mightier enemy. There are many other examples like this starting from the antiquity, the Middle Ages until the present time in all parts of the world. You can make an experiment - choose any country in the world and read its short history. You will see that most countries and regions have a drastic difference in their former and current ethnic composition which means that the past ethnical groups were replaced with new ones. Sadly, this is the way mankind functions. But is anyone mentioning all of these other examples of ethnical cleaning? Why do many people today stress only the Americans and the tragic destiny of the Indians without even mentioning other numerous similar cases in the history? Isn't this again an example of the anti-USA propaganda?

2.1.4. Mediums overstating certain missteps of the US administration

If someone from the US administration accidentally infringes a human right (which is common in every country), then such an event gets a wide media attention in many countries. One of the many examples regarding this is an event from my country Republic of Macedonia. At the end of 2003 in Macedonia, a German citizen with Arabian ethnic background named Khalid El-Masri was wrongfully arrested by the Macedonian police. The reason for the arrest was that he had an identical name with an Al-Qaeda activist. Khalid El-Masri was given away to CIA that secretly sent him to Afghanistan where (according to his claiming) he was inquired and physically abused. Later on, the mistake was realized and he was released in May 2004. Even though according to some mediums this Khalid El-Masri was really an Islamic extremist, we should agree that the Macedonian police and the CIA made a mistake in this case. This misstep cannot be justified, although the USA is first on the list when it comes to Islamic terrorism, so their wariness is understandable. However, sometimes mistakes like this happened and can be mended by legal arrangements.

But, what happened later? The wrongfully kidnapping of Khalid El-Masri became a trending topic in lots of European and Macedonian media. The anti-USA propagandists gained more "food" to bite on, so this event was talked about for years with, of course, always accenting the "wrong kidnapping by the CIA". Again, I am not against justified criticism on the mistakes made by the US administration, but why so much noise on this case? How many people are kidnapped almost every day? At the exact same time, many soldiers, civilians, natives, both men and women were kidnapped in the

Russian area of Chechnya. Did the media put such attention on them as they did for the kidnapping of El-Masri? In 2005, three poor Macedonian workers were kidnapped in Iraq and savagely executed by the Islamic terrorists. In 2006 four more Macedonian workers with Albanian ethnicity were kidnapped and killed by the Taliban in Afghanistan. Besides in Macedonia, did any of the European media say anything about these kidnappings (even though they both ended tragically)? Instead, they continued talking and talking only about the Khalid El-Masri case, although his kidnapping had a happy end.

The European institutions also organized a session for the kidnapping of El-Masri, and Macedonia was publicly accused of helping the CIA. However, we did not see these same European institutions organizing sessions for the kidnappings and murders of the poor Macedonian citizens in Iraq and Afghanistan.

What is the reason behind all this? It is clear that the reason is– the USA! If the USA is involved in a kidnapping (which, again, ended with a happy end), then attack the USA every day in the media! Isn't this a pure example of the anti-USA propaganda in which this time were involved some frustrated Western-Europeans?

I will say one more thing about the absurdity of all of this. In the moment of writing this text, I searched Khalid El-Masri on Google and around 1,410.000 web-pages appeared. Of course, some may not be connected to the person we talked about, but the bigger part of these web-pages (including the first ranked) are without doubt dedicated to this kidnapping. Then I searched the words "kidnapping Chechnya". Believe it or not, "only" 1.060.000 appeared. This means that there is a lot more information about the wrongfully kidnapping of Khalid El-Masri (which ended with a happy end) than the tragic kidnappings in Chechnya in which many people have lost their lives! Here were included kidnappings of foreign workers, Russian soldiers, Chechnya civilians and activists, and young Chechnya girls who are still kidnapped and forced to marry. All of these hundreds of kidnappings with their tragic ends seem not so "important" as the Khalid El-Masri case. I will not talk about kidnappings from other parts of the world (especially in Nigeria made by a terrorist organization Boko Haram), but I will just say that this is another typical example of hate and frustrations against the USA.

2.1.5. Wikileaks

Let's say something in short about the Wikileaks affair. We will not write much about its character because it is enough to look at the statistic information about the number of the so far released documents by this organization. These "leaks" are in largest majority connected only with the USA, which means that no matter how this organization declares itself, they are operating on an anti-USA basis.

2.1.6. Accusing the USA of being the "worlds policeman"

Many people are accusing the USA of being a "world policeman" in a negative connotation. I am really confused when anti-USA propagandists use this kind of qualification. It is a simple logic that the word "policeman" implies a potential criminal around. And if there is criminal around i.e. endangered safety, then it is normal to have the need of policemen. Everywhere in the world (except maybe in the totalitarian regimes) the police is considered in a positive context (a group that protects people), but I guess this does not apply to the anti-USA propagandists. The "police" obviously has negative connotation in their ravage logic – something the psychologists should take a look at.

Qualifying the USA as a "world policeman" is somewhat correct, but in a positive sense. Namely, it is a fact that the military power of the USA is the biggest rampart against the most aggressive military-extreme, planetary ideological determinations: the military Islamic fundamentalism and communism. I ask every well-meaning person to think about what will the world become if the USA were not what they are now? Who will oppose the militant Islam that is publicly spread in some countries? Who will oppose the communism, which still remains undefeated?

Today millions of people across the world are barely aware that their safety is guarded directly or indirectly by the USA. In one conversation with an anti-NATO Australian, I asked him: "Are you afraid that one day Indonesia may attack Australia?" He confusingly looked at me asking "How can you even think about something like that? That is nonsense. That is impossible". I said: "You are right, it really is impossible, but do you know why? It is because NATO and the USA are backing Australia and that is why you the Australians are safe from external aggression. Think of a situation in which the USA is not so powerful and NATO does not exist – Australia will be left alone in their defense. Imagine if the Islamic extremists, in certain circumstances, will come to power in Indonesia. Who will defend you then? Then I explained that external aggression towards Australia is not an unreal scenario, because Japan in the World War two had the exact plan as part of their strategic goal – to occupy Australia and colonize it with Japanese. It was possible in that time since the USA was not as powerful as it is today. These kind of potential examples are many, and that is why hundreds of millions of people should be thankful to the USA since they are the strongest defender of the free

28

democratic world against the totalitarian invasion. If someone says that the USA is not a "democratic country" then I suggest them to take a look at their own country first, then criticizing others.

In the end I would like to state that when I say "Islamic extremism" I by any means do not identify it with the Islam. On the contrary, I deeply respect Islam as a religion that preaches love and respect among people. I have read the Holy Quran and have quoted parts of it in some of my books. My opinion is that Christianity, Judaism and Islam (as well as the other religions) should fraternally cooperate, pointing out their common values such as: the existence of God, the existence of the afterlife and making good deeds on the earthly life in order to be rewarded in the afterlife. I respect all religions, even though I serve God as an Orthodox believer. When I mentioned "Islamic extremism", I meant the people who kill innocents in the name of Islam – something that is strictly forbidden in the Islam itself, even though such extremists exist in other religions as well (including Christianity).

2.2. Using (abusing) the USA superiority in science

This form of anti-USA propaganda mainly founds its base among the less educated and uninformed people whose number is not small, especially in the Third World countries. The main form of this activity is a production of the conspiracy theories which base is directly connected with the superiority of the USA in many science fields.

From the area of distribution aspect, this form of anti-USA propaganda can be: a) regional and b) local;

a) The regional distribution of the anti-USA articulations implicates the USA for generally-known negative events and occurrences, which happen in different regions of the world or even worldwide. There is a transmission of information in which the same information with anti-USA context is translated into many languages and distributed in various countries and regions (more examples will be given).

b) The local distribution of the articulations with anti-USA propaganda is about accusing the USA for the negative events and occurrences that appear in some local community. In these cases, the distribution of information with anti-USA context is usually limited to the country only, or the impacted region (more examples will be given).

There are number of examples for **regional distribution of the anti-USA articulations.** Nowadays, the anti-USA propagandists accuse the USA for almost all natural disasters or any kind of accidents that the mankind faces. Here are some characteristic examples:

1. *The Americans invented the HIV virus.* Numerous claims regarding this can be found on the internet or in the electronic and written media. These claims manipulate with data (in order to be more plausible) and try to convince the public that there are "proofs" or even "confessions" by some Americans that the HIV virus is created in the USA (some are blaming the CIA, others the Pentagon).

2. *The Americans created the avian influenza in order to produce and sell vaccines.* From the numerous examples of these statements, we will share the statement from Lorraine Day, just as an illustration: http://www.goodnewsaboutgod.com/studies/birdflu_mutation.htm

3. *The Americans invented the SARS virus to destroy the Chinese who begun to economically imperil the USA.* Examples on

this statement can be found around the internet.

4. *Americans are responsible for the creation of the Ebola virus.* These claims can also be found on the internet by anyone. Here is one made in the dictatorship communist regime of North Korea - http://www.washingtonpost.com/blogs/worldvie ws/wp/2014/12/01/north-korea-says-u-s-created-the-ebola-outbreak/

5. *Using the HAARP system in 2014, the Americans caused floods in Serbia, Croatia and Bosnia and Herzegovina. Using this system, they caused all the major natural catastrophes including the tsunami in 2004.* These mad affirmations are presented by two Russian researchers: Sokolov Alexei Vyeceslavovic and Burmakin Alexei Leonidovic in their text named "Geophysical-climate weapon – has the war already begun?" published in Russian http://www.rusidea.org/?a=34009, and then translated into Serbian and other languages and then widely spread across the internet. The authors Vyeceslavovic and Leonidovic (obviously members of the firm military line filled with hatred against the USA) are candidates of military studies. In their text (in which they quote "some researchers or war experts" without putting their names), the authors (without any proofs) claim that HAARP was used long before and that is the reason for all the cataclysms in Europe and the world since 1997. They present a list of the cataclysms that (according to their "sources") were caused by the USA:

- *The hurricane "El Nino" (1997-1998) which caused damage of 20 billion dollars.*

31

- *The 1999 earthquake in Turkey with 7.6 degrees strength, ending 20,000 lives.*
- *The hurricane "Isabel" in 2003 which ended thousands of lives.*
- *The tsunami in 2004, ending 300,000 lives.*
- *The 2005 earthquake in Pakistan with 7.6 degrees strength, ending 100.000 lives.*
- *The activation of the Chaiten volcano in Chile in 2008.*
- *The activation of the Island volcano in 2010.*

Vyeceslavovic and Leonodovic continue their text saying that the USA made climate experiments over Russia, reminding us that during those two months, the temperature in Moscow was like in the Libyan Desert or Sahara. And that's not all. Americans with their climate weapon were also responsible for:

- Potential major accident hazard of the Russian plane TU 153 and his forced landing on September 7th 2010.

- Series of unsuccessful launchings of the new Russian ballistic rockets "Bulava", placed on the sea coast of the equivalent geographical latitude on the north hemisphere.

There are many other similar accusations against "the Americans" who are accused for almost all evilness in the world. In my country there is a female journalist (an openly declared leftist) that has pathological hatred towards the USA in her writings. Mention any affair in recent history from any part of the world (an unsolved political assassination, a big traffic accident, a natural disaster, an epidemic etc.) and this americanophobic journalist will immediately provide "evidence" that this affair is a "deed of the CIA".

Here we enunciated only the most important ones that are widely used by the anti-USA provocateurs on a global level.

The largest part of the well-informed and objective

readers should laugh at these affirmations. Unlike them, there are USA-haters who do not consider arguments, but only have a blind hate towards the USA. These people are not even worth for discussion. In fact, these people are the ones who produce these accusations and spread them across the media or the internet. However, there is a third group of readers which is the largest, and those are the ones who are not adept enough into all this, so some of them may think about the authenticity of these accusations by the anti-USA provocateurs. This group is the main reason why we will explain some of these above-mentioned accusations. Spreading misinformation in order to create more USA enemies is the main aim of these anti-USA propagandists, and should no one replies to this misinformation – some might start to believe that they are true.

1. We will start with the accusations about the USA creating the HIV virus in order to "destroy whole nations" (some provocateurs say that Americans invented this virus to destroy "black people"). For the sake of space, we will point out only a few universally accepted facts.

It is widely accepted by the serious scientists from all over the world that the HIV virus originates from some species of monkeys from middle-west Africa and that the roots of this disease date back since the late 19th and the early 20th century. Science has already identified the few species of monkeys that carry the HIV virus which, after consuming their meat by the local community, was transmitted into the people. This data are widely known and accepted by the serious scientific public and wider. As an illustration, we will state a few extracts regarding the origin of the HIV virus from probably the most well-known Russian web-site about the battle against aids – www.aids.ru:

"Besides availability of greater number of genetic subspecies of a HIV in African comparison with all other

33

continents, testifies that the virus already long time occurs among the African population and accordingly changes.(...) Leading virologist Jaap Gudsmit considers that the area of Africa where the HIV likely first appeared is Cameroon and the western equatorial coast, as it is unique area in Africa where today find a HIV-1, a HIV-2 and rather new subspecies (subtype) of a HIV-1 - a HIV-0. It considers, that propagation of subspecies of a HIV from this region could begin in the beginning of the twentieth century that was probably promoted by commerce between Cameroon and Tanganyika"

Direct or indirect collaborators of this Russian website are famous Russian experts on AIDS, whose names are mentioned on the website.

Maliciously claiming that the Americans created the HIV virus is not only refuted by science, but refuted by logic itself. Namely, according the data from 2012, there are 4,600,000 people who died from AIDS, 642,000 of which are Americans. If the USA created this virus to "destroy" other nations, would they let a number of victims as this in their own country? Can a normal person believe such a thing?

2. As for the avian influenza and the accusations that the USA created it, we will quote an extract from the official statement of the World Health Organization where it is clearly stated that the virus of this influenza comes from livestock in China and was transmitted to people by eating their meat. Regarding this, the official website of the WHO states:

"Avian influenza A(H7N9) is a subtype of influenza viruses that have been detected in birds in the past. This particular A(H7N9) virus had not previously been seen in either animals or people until it was found in March 2013 in China.

However, since then, infections in both humans and birds have been observed. The disease is of concern because most patients have become severely ill.

Most of the cases of human infection with this avian H7N9 virus have reported recent exposure to live poultry or potentially contaminated environments, especially markets where live birds have been sold. This virus does not appear to transmit easily from person to person, and sustained human-to-human transmission has not been reported."

Then:

"Since the first notification at the end of March 2013, China has been reporting to WHO cases of human infection with H7N9virus. This is the first time infection with this virus has been found in humans.

The laboratory-confirmed cases have been reported from 13 provinces/municipalities in eastern mainland China, Hong Kong, Special Administrative Region, China, and the Taipei Centers for Disease Control (Taipei CDC). Most cases are presumed to have contracted the infection directly from infected animals or their environment, particularly as a result of visiting live animal markets.

(...)

Thus far the H7N9 viruses detected in China are homologues. The HA gene is most similar to that of A(H7N3) viruses detected in ducks in Eastern China. The NA gene is most similar to N9 NA genes from viruses circulating recently in domestic ducks in China and Korea. The six internal genes are derived from influenza A(H9N2) viruses circulating in poultry in eastern Asia. Sequence analyses have shown that the genes of the H7N9 viruses from China are of avian origin, but with signs of adaptation to mammalian species. (http: //www.who.int/influenza/human_animal_interface/201401 31_background_and_summary_H7N9_v1.pdf?ua=1)"

It is worth mentioning that the director of the World Health Organization is Dr. Margaret Chan from China.

Additional comments for refuting this anti-USA provocation are not needed.

3. Regarding the accusations that the Americans created the SARS virus, we will point out a few universally accepted facts that anyone can check out.

- Firstly, it is proven that the SARS virus is from animal origin and this can be read in every serious medical publication.

- Secondly, the SARS epidemic first appeared in China, concretely in the Chinese province of Guangdong in November 2002. Shortly after that, the first victims were reported. But China informed the World Health Organization about this epidemic only in February 2003. The Chinese authorities have hid this epidemic from the rest of the world for three months, and they received a criticism from the World Health Organization. In April 2003, Chinese government officially indicated an apology about its behavior. The reasons for hiding this epidemic can only be guessed, but it is sure that they would not have hid the epidemic had someone "brought it" from the outside, as the anti-USA provocateurs claim.

- It is a fact that (because of the reasons this virus exists are from China) most citizens who died from this illness are from China (a total of 648 including Hong Kong). But, in second place in terms of victims is Canada with 44. How would the anti-USA provocateurs explain this? Has the USA (besides "hating" China) spread the virus in Canada because they "hate" them too?

- Finally, the Chinese themselves admitted that the SARS epidemic originated in their country, i.e. it appeared in Guangdong as a result of eating a civet cat's meat that contained this virus. As a proof of this, I will mention the official report written by the Chinese scientists from the Chinese Centre for Disease Control and Prevention, Hong Kong University and the Guangzhou Centre for Disease Control and Prevention, which was published in the edition of "China Daily" on 26.11.2006.

In this report the Chinese authors clearly indicate

that the civet cat's meat, which contained the SARS virus, was served in Guangdong restaurants and that is how it was transmitted to people.

"China Daily" stated that a group of scientists announced that a research team had found a genetic link between the SARS corona virus appearing in civet cats and humans. Then followed the names of the scientific faculties that participated in this research and the declaration of Wang Ming, an official from the Guangzhou Centre for Disease Control and Prevention in which he points out that their research demonstrated that the SARS corona virus found in human victims is the same as the SARS corona virus found in civet cats.

In addition, Wang stated that this discovery offered proofs that civet cats had spread SARS to humans.

From Wang's statement we can also see that the SARS infection was noticed in civet casts at an animal market. He explains that the scientists brought civet cats from the restaurant to the laboratory, where tests proved that the disease the animals carried had the same genetic profile as the corona virus affecting the SARS patient (more on this on "China Daily", 23 November 2006).

It really is unscrupulous that the anti-USA provocateurs want to benefit from every humanitarian disaster (in this case the SARS epidemic in China and other countries).

4. As for the accusations that Americans created the Ebola virus, it would be enough to quote a statement from the World Health Organization's website in patronage of the United Nations, in which 194 countries are members and as we mentioned, the general director is Dr. Margaret Chan from China. On their official website, regarding the creation of the Ebola virus, it is clearly stated that it is from animal origin, i.e. it comes from a certain type of bat and that initially appeared in

Africa:

"*Ebola first appeared in 1976 in two simultaneous outbreaks, one in a village near the Ebola River in the Democratic Republic of Congo, and the other in a remote area of Sudan. The origin of the virus is unknown but fruit bats (Pteropodidae) are considered the likely host of the Ebola virus, based on available evidence.*(http://www.who.int/csr/disease/ebola/faq-ebola/en/).

Further comments are not needed, except one more reminding of the unscrupulousness of the anti-USA provocateurs who obviously have a sense of dark humor, claiming that the USA is "obsessed" with "creating viruses" for destroying the poor people in Africa (although they never made any harm to USA) and not for destroying the real enemies of the USA.

Later on, we will mention another thing about the USA contribution in the medicine and the battle for suppressing the epidemics from deadly diseases.

5. Now let's take a look on the accusations according to which the Americans used the HAARP system to cause floods in Serbia, Croatia and Bosnia and Herzegovina in 2014. I shall start with an anecdote. In the summer 2014 the weather was really rainy in my country, Republic of Macedonia, and in my city. There were floods in the nearby countries of Serbia, Croatia and Bosnia and Herzegovina in which about eighty people lost their lives. At work, we discussed about this with my colleagues and the woman cleaner suddenly said: "*Look what those Americans have done to us with their HAARP system*". I looked at her with surprise and asked: "*What have they done?*" She answered unsurely: "*They changed our climate… That is the reason for the Serbia floods*". I asked: "*Do you know what HAARP is?*", and she said without even thinking:"*No… No idea*". I reacted with: "*If you have no idea, how do you know that HAARP is the reason for the floods?*". She became even

more uncertain and started to back up saying *"I heard some people saying this"*...

This conversation with the woman cleaner is a typical example which refers to anyone who thinks that the HAARP system brought climate changes in Europe and was the reason of the Balkan floods. Make an inquiry and ask people who believe this nonsense - how many of them actually know what HAARP is? I guarantee that 99,9% would have no idea. So how can they claim something without even having the basic knowledge about it?

But the anti-USA propagandists used the lack of knowledge of the people and they forced the HAARP story. To make the story more "believable" they found some seemingly "experts" who "professionally" claimed that "the HAARP system caused climate changes in the Balkan and brought a rainy summer in 2014, resulting in massive floods in Serbia, Croatia and Bosnia and Herzegovina".

This form of manipulation with people sometimes reached tragicomic levels. On Facebook, a Macedonian profile by an anonymous provocateur appeared that was followed by many dupes. One of their posts was that in a city in Macedonia, "mysterious antennas" appeared around buildings and "people in black speaking English" were hanging around them (!?). The message is clear: *evil Americans came to Macedonia (dressed in black) to put antennas so that HAARP can spoil our climate and cause floods as those in Serbia.*

The dupes who believed in these HAARP provocations (which for the first time appeared on the Balkan in Serbian and Russian language with quotes from some Russian "expert") did not ask themselves why neither one serious media outlet (private or state-owned) from Macedonia or Serbia reported such nonsense? Why did serious experts from Macedonia or Serbia, who were guests on the media and actually knew what HAARP is (unlike the above mentioned woman cleaner), say that it is nonsense to claim that HAARP is the reason for the rainy summer and the floods?

Besides this, there are still some unanswered questions.

1. If the American HAARP program caused floods in Serbia, Bosnia and Herzegovina and Croatia, then who caused the floods in Europe and the rest of the world before the existence of the HAARP? Let the anti-USA provocateurs answer this simple question. In the history of the world, there have been thousands of floods with numerous victims. The reasons were different, but usually centered around heavy rains. Who caused the flood in Valencia (Spain) in 1957 which ended 81 lives? Who caused the flood in England in the far 1287 which ended thousands of lives? Or the floods in England in 1738, 1777, 1825, 1852, 1864, 1928, 1944, 1947 and many more, also resulting in a huge number of victims? Maybe the Americans used time machine to bring their HAARP in the past and cause floods to their closest ally? But, if the Americans really caused every flood in the world, then who caused the big floods in the USA itself in 1740, 1785, 1786, 1800, 1806, 1811, 1814, 1832, 1904, 1905, 1906, 1907, 1908, 1911, 1913, 1927, 1936 and tens or even hundreds smaller or bigger ones which also resulted in a big number of victims? There is not a single country in the world (beside those in the dry regions) that was not hit by a flood several times during the history, so it is a notorious nonsense to claim that, among the thousands of floods, only the floods in Serbia were caused by the HAARP system. Instead of believing such nonsense, it would be the best for anyone to educate himself and learn what HAARP is and not from some suspicious sources, but from the relevant scientific institutions in their country.

This way they won't end up as a victim and an experimental guinea-pig of the malicious anti-USA provocateurs.

Speaking of the scientific experiments connected with the ionosphere, I will ask one more question: Why is everyone only talking about the USA HAARP? Why is everyone barely mentioning the Russian "HAARP" (named "Sura Ionospheric Heating Facility")? Many have no idea that Russia has a similar system for a lot longer than the Americans (more details on their official website http://sura.nirfi.scinnov.ru/page2.html?height=2000&source=ExperimentalResults/News.html). The Russian Ionospheric Heating Facility was found in 1981(The American HAARP started in 1993) and its location is near the small town of Vasilsursk, 100 km east of Nizhny Novgorod. A logical question for the anti-USA provocateurs: Is the Russian "HAARP" responsible for the floods from 1981 till today? There are Americans who argue that the hurricane Katrina that hit New Orleans in 2005 and took over 700 lives was an act of a secret Russian meteorological weapon. The American meteorologist Scott Stevens accused Russia of creating the Katrina hurricane. The supporters of Scott Stevens are reminding us of an interview in which the Russian ultra-nationalist and an opposition politician Vladimir Zhirinovsky warned USA of massive floods as a result of the changes in Earth's gravitational field caused by secret Russian experiments. According to Stevens, these Russian experiments of changing the climate date back since the era of the Soviet Union (USSR) (http://www.bibliotecapleyades.net/haarp/esp_HAARP_27.htm).

But, the truth is that both the Russian and the American system are used for scientific purposes and anyone who believes differently is a naive victim of manipulation.

Now back to the previous topic. We will give answers to the fake accusations made by the previously mentioned Russian authors. We chose the text from these two authors as an illustration not only because it is widespread, but because it contains a wide pallet of accusations against the USA. There are of course other authors who support these accusations, so these answers are to all of them. Let's start from the beginning. According to the claims presented in the text of the two Russian authors, the USA using the HAARP system generated (quote) *"the hurricane El Nino"* in 1997-1998 that hit many cities and caused 20 billion dollars in damage. We will immediately say that this argument is a notorious lie! Firstly, there is no hurricane named "El Nino", so these Russian authors either made a serious oversight or have lack of basic knowledge! Anyone willing to search can check through professional literature and see that *"El Niño is the warm phase of the El Nino Southern Oscillation (commonly called ENSO) and is associated with a band of warm ocean water that develops in the central and east-central equatorial Pacific, including off the Pacific coast of South America. El Nino Southern Oscillation refers to the cycle of warm and cold temperatures, as measured by sea surface temperature SST, of the tropical central and eastern Pacific Ocean. El Niño is accompanied by high air pressure in the western Pacific and low air pressure in the eastern Pacific. The cool phase of ENSO is called "La Niña" with SST in the eastern Pacific below average and air pressures high in the eastern and low in western Pacific. The ENSO cycle, both El Niño and La Niña, causes global changes of both temperatures and rainfall. Mechanisms that cause the oscillation remain under study"* (from http://en.wikipedia.org/wiki/El_Ni%C3%B1o K.E. Trenberth, P.D. Jones, P. Ambenje, R. Bojariu , D. Easterling, A. Klein Tank, D. Parker, F. Rahimzadeh, J.A. Renwick, M. Rusticucci, B. Soden and P. Zhai. "Observations: Surface and Atmospheric Climate Change". In Solomon, S., D. Qin, M. Manning, Z. Chen, M. Marquis, K.B. Averyt, M. Tignor and H.L. Miller.

Climate Change 200 7, The Physical Science Basis Contribution of Working Group I to the Fourth Assessment Report of the Inter governmental Panel on Climate Change, Cambridge, UK: Cambridge University Press. pp. 235–336.)

No one can foresee the change in temperature on a global level. For example, in February 2014 a group of German meteorologists foresaw that the climate phenomenon "El Nino" will bring a very hot summer in 2014 (the news from the German meteorologists were published on some Macedonian websites). But in fact, the very opposite happened (at least in the bigger part of Europe) – the summer was pretty cold and rainy.

Actually, the climate phenomenon El Nino happens every two to seven years since the early history of the Earth. There is recorded information of this climate phenomenon having stronger effects in the years 1789, 1876, 1892, 1924 etc. All of this happened before the existence of HAARP, so the claims of the anonymous "sources" who are used by the Russian authors according to which the hurricane "El Nino" was caused by the HAARP system are not only fictitious, but senseless too.

Regarding the statement that the Americans using the HAARP system caused the 1999 earthquake in Turkey with a magnitude of 7.6 degrees and ending 20,000 lives, we will say that it is not only malicious, but insulting to the victims and their families too. It really is inhuman to play games with such tragedies. But, let's get back to the facts. A big part of Turkey is seismological a quake territory where dozens of strong earthquakes have happened throughout the history. The most deadly one was in the antique, year 115, and it is estimated that around 260,000 died in the city of Antioch and its surrounding. Antioch was again hit in year 526 with 250,000 victims. Strong earthquakes on the Turkey territory with a magnitude of above 7 degrees happened in: Istanbul (1509), Smyrna (1653), Anatolia and again Smyrna (1668), Istanbul and Izmir (1894), Mürefte (1912), Erzincan (1939), Erba (1942), Ladik (1943), Gerede (1944), Yenikent (1953), Fethiye (1953), Abant (1957), Manias (1964), Mudurnu (1967), Gediz (1970), Muradiye (1976), Izmir (1999), Düzce (1999) and Van (2011). Tens of thousands people have died in all of these exclusively strong earthquakes. There is also data for dozens of earthquakes with a magnitude of above 6 degrees that happened throughout the history, since the Middle ages to the present days in which thousands of people have also died. There are even hundreds of earthquakes below 6 degrees because of the quake territory on which Turkey is located. One must be out of their mind to claim that all these hundreds of earthquakes in Turkey were caused by nature, and only the 1999 one (in Izmir, and not in Duzke which happened the same year) was caused by the HAARP system. There is no need of reminding us that Turkey is one of the most loyal allies of the USA, so if HAARP was used as a "secret weapon", it would have been used against the American enemies, not allies.

- According to the claims presented in the Russian author's text, the USA using HAARP created the hurricane "Isabel" in 2003 that took (quote) "few thousands lives". This claim is without doubt among the biggest gaffes from the above-mentioned anti-American pamphlet. Hurricane "Isabel" (originating in the Atlantic Ocean) hit the USA in 2003 and mainly people in Virginia, Florida, North Carolina, West Virginia, the capital city Washington DC, Maryland, Pennsylvania, New York and other areas perished as a result. There were victims and damages in millions of dollars. Let's get back to the title of the Russian author's pamphlet: "Geophysical-climate weapon – has the war already begun?" This title implies that the Americans have started a "war" already using their "Geophysical-climate

44

weapon". But all the wars in the world are against a certain enemy. No one ever has led a war against themselves, and this pamphlet is saying that the Americans using the "Geophysical-climate weapon" declared war on themselves and hit none other than their own capital city (if we have in mind that the hurricane "Isabel" also hit Washington DC.). I admit, I have never read bigger nonsense than this and I really ponder about the mentality of the people who believe in these tragic-comical articulations. But that's not all. We also read that the number of Americans who lost their lives as a result of "Isabel" was "few thousands". This is far from the truth. Only 16 people died during the hurricane, and 35 as a result of the indirect consequences, which means that the overall number of victims from "Isabel" was 51, not "few thousands". Finally, the US government using the media warned the citizen days before the hurricane appeared, so safety precautions were taken and this is how the number of victims was reduced. Knowing this, the arguments of the Russian authors become even more absurd. According to them, the USA, using the hurricane "Isabel," led war against them-selves, but first warned their citizens to take precautions from this "American weapon."

Let's say a few words about the tsunami in 2004. It really is inhumane to manipulate the victims of one of the biggest natural disasters that happened to humanity, by indirectly accusing Americans of taking their lives. The epicenter of the strong underwater earthquake that caused the tsunami happened nearby the Indonesian island Sumatra, and countries that suffered the most were Indonesia, Sri Lanka, India, Thailand, Somalia, Myanmar, Maldives, Malaysia, Tanzania, Seychelles, Bangladesh, South African Republic, Yemen, Kenya, Madagascar and others. It is estimated that around 280.000 people lost their lives and it is considered one of the biggest natural disasters in the history. It is tragic that

these poor countries were hit without defense systems that could mitigate the deadly tsunami. The whole world showed harmony and the USA donated hundreds of millions dollars in help (around 950 million USD, according the official sources). Other countries have also helped. My small country, the Republic of Macedonia (with around 2 million citizens) has managed to donate around 2 million USD. China donated 80 million USD to the countries struck, Austria donated 65 million USD, Denmark 74 million USD, France around 303 million USD, Germany 673 million USD, Greece 1,7 million USD, India 183 million USD, Japan 500 million USD, Kuwait 100 million USD, Holland 300 million USD, Saudi Arabia 60 million USD, Great Britain 145 million USD, Turkey 29 million USD etc. Over 50 countries gathered and donated financial aid to those struck by the tsunami. An interesting fact is that Russia donated only around 2 million USD which is same as my country, Macedonia, even though Russia has 72 times more population than Macedonia. In his text "Russia Contributes $2M to Tsunami Fund" published in "The Moscow Times" (11.01.2005), the Russian journalist Nabi Abdullaev writes that the relatively small amount of Russia's contribution provoked criticism from some Western politicians. Abdullaev writes that Russia's $2 million is less than some individual contributions whereupon reminding us that Michael Schumacher donated $10 million, Hollywood director Steven Spielberg donated $1.5 million and the actress Sandra Bullock donated $1 million.
(http://www.themoscowtimes.com/news/article/russia-contributes-2m-to-tsunami-fund/225990.html).

But, let's go back to the facts about the tsunami phenomenon. We will not explain here how a tsunami is created since there are a lot of scientific explanations that anyone can find and read. We will stress one notorious truth: tsunamis have been registered since early history. There is data for around 70 tsunamis appearing from the prehistoric era. Knowing this, it becomes absurd to claim that every tsunami that happened so far is naturally caused, but only the 2004 tsunami was "caused" by the USA (even though this country helped the most to the poor struck countries and even though these statements are backed by no proofs, except malicious fabrications).

It is the same case with the claim that the USA caused the 2005 earthquake in Pakistan. Every reader can see for himself that the Pakistan territory, like Turkey, is located on a quake area and one of the biggest fissures in Asia is passing right through their whole territory. Because of this, many earthquakes have appeared since ancient history, some of which were disastrous. The biggest and most powerful earthquake happened between in 893 and it is said that around 150.000 people lost their lives. It is estimated that the magnitude of this earthquake was 8 degrees on the Richter's scale. Strong earthquakes on the territory of the present days' Pakistan have also appeared in: 1668 (50.000 victims), 1819 (3,200 victims), 1827 (1,000 victims), 1852, 1865, 1883, 1889, 1892, 1909, 1929, 1931 (two earthquakes), 1935 (30,000 to 60,000 victims), 1945, 1974 and so on. Knowing these tragic facts, I ask the anti-USA provocateurs to answer who caused these deadly earthquakes? Can a normal person believe that all these earthquakes happened as a result of the Pakistan's quake area, while only the 2005 one happened because of the Americans?

The claim that the Americans caused the eruption of the Chaitén volcano in Chile is also nonsense. It is clear that no matter where the eruption happened, the Americans would have been accused by the anti-American provocateurs. As for Chile, believe it or not, it is a country with around 500 volcanoes, 123 of which are active and each of them had at least one eruption in the past millennium. I hope that no one will say that the Americans using their "secret time machine" transported the HAARP system into the past and caused all these volcanic eruptions or other natural catastrophes.

Even more senseless is the claim that in 2010, the Americans purposely caused the eruption on the volcano in Iceland which resulted in many flights being canceled. Many European countries, mostly Norway and Great Britain suffered heavy damage in the air transport. Essentially, the anti-American provocateurs claim that the USA attacked the economy of their most loyal ally, Great Britain, using their "climate weapon" which "activated" the volcano in Iceland. One must be out of his mind to believe this.

As for the claims that the Americans caused the major accident of the Russian plane TU 153 and its forced landing on September 7th 2010, as well as others accusations about the unsuccessful launchings of the new ballistic rockets "Bulava," I call both Russian authors who claim this to ask construction workers and airplane and rocket engineers for the mistakes they have made. These mistakes can happen to airplanes and rockets in the USA and other countries too. Other comments regarding this folly statement are not needed.

A few words on **the regional distribution** of the anti-USA articulations:

We will illustrate this using an exact example from Republic of Macedonia.

Some local electronic media outlets were hoaxed by Americanophobes with false information about a "radioactive material" buried, without the Macedonian government knowing, from the Americans in the Macedonian region of Krivolak (a region where marines were living for a while and military exercises were performed together with the Macedonian forces) and that this whole region became "radioactive". One local TV

48

station even brought a semi-literate old aged villager who publicly claimed that since his arrival in this region, "redness" has appeared on his hand.

The next day experts from the regional Mining department went out and publicly showed that their Geiger counter showed no signs of radiation. However, individual anti-American fanatics continued to claim that there is radiation that "cannot be traced with Geiger counters." They did not say how they managed to trace this radiation, so obviously it existed only in their heads.

We will mention another example from 2014 that is well known in the world. On the 8th of March, the Malaysian airplane with flight number 370 disappeared with all its passengers and crew and still hasn't been found by the time of writing this text. This mysterious tragedy was again an opportunity for the anti-USA provocateurs to act. Some of the websites from my country published an article (translated from English) by some freelance journalist named Jim Stone that he wrote for the Australian internet-edition of "International Business Times" (This theory can be found on many other web-pages including: http://au.ibtimes.com/articles/547244/20140409/mh370-diego-garcia-found-conspiracy-theory gps.htm#.VHMaC01AS2x).

According to Jim Stone, a passenger named Philip Wood from the missing Malaysian airplane sent a message from his phone (iPhone 5) saying that he was held hostage and drugged after the airplane was hijacked.

Stone claims that according to the GPS coordinates found from the moment of sending the message, Wood was a few miles away from the American secret military base "Diego Garcia" located on an island south of Maldives in the Indian Ocean.

This means that according to this theory, the Americans, for mysterious reasons, hijacked the

Malaysian airplane and forced it to land in their secret military base from where a passenger sent an SMS message to the journalist Stone, who is known for dealing with conspiracy theories. The author of this anti-USA provocation forgot at least two details. Firstly, if the airplane was hijacked by the American army, they would have thoroughly searched every passenger. How did the respective Philip Wood manage to hide his cell phone and keep it hidden for 11 days? The journalist Stone claims that the passenger wrote that he hid his iPhone 5 in, believe it or not – his anus! Imagine someone shoving his phone with 4.87 inches height (12.38 cm) and 2.31 inches width (5.86 cm) in his anus while sitting on his seat in the plane. Even if we consider this true, Stone forgot another, even bigger detail. Namely, it is known that the Malaysian airplane disappeared on 8th March and the SMS message was allegedly sent on 18th March, meaning 11 days after the disappearing ("hijacking"). It is also known that the battery of an iPhone 5 can last for seven days at most, if the phone is idle. So the question for Stone and other provocateurs is: how did the battery of the kidnapped passenger last for so long without being charged? Did he charge it in his anus? This is the level of stupidity that the anti-USA propaganda can sometimes reach. Some of these provocateurs are literally underestimating the intelligence of the readers by presenting such nonsense as this. Not only this, but they also abused the name of the unfortunate passenger Wood, who without his fault, is unscrupulously used in this insolent articulation of the anti-USA propaganda.

From the so-far presented, we see that the scheme of such accusations is the same and happens in the following order:
1. An epidemic of a deadly disease appears somewhere in the world;
2. It is waited for a period to see if the reasons for

this disease are known or unknown;

3. If the scientists cannot immediately discover the reasons for the epidemic, then the anti-USA conspirators (some of which are Americans) start to sell their theories that "the USA are behind the virus and the epidemic" and is created under the command of CIA or a military authority in their "secret laboratories".

4. If the victims from the epidemic are mainly citizens from another nation, then "the Americans created this virus to destroy that nation". If Americans or citizens from their allied countries also suffer, then it is explained as a "mistake in estimation" or a "collateral damage"... All to the point when another epidemic appears, then this scheme is repeated. Grand-scaled natural disasters are also "explained" using this scheme.

Common segments for these propagandistic articulations are the following:

- Using (abusing) the USA superiority in certain fields of science, notions connected with advanced science are used, which are in practice in the USA, but not in other countries where the anti-USA propaganda is spread. For example, when "secret laboratories" are mentioned and they only exist in the USA for various scientific researches, but they do not exist in the Third world countries; then the "radioactive energy" that the USA use, but not the Third world countries; "viruses created in laboratories" – something unimaginable in the Third world countries, but "possible" only in the USA etc.

- Lack of knowledge and insufficient education of a large number of people in relation with scientific fields. Resultantly, an average citizen from the Third world countries does not have even elementary knowledge of atomic physics or modern medicine. This lack of knowledge is abused by selling unfamiliar notions to the ordinary people, whose mentioning sounds fearful (*radiation, viruses* etc.).

- Conspiracy. The superiority of the USA in science together with the existing disasters that humanity faces (diseases or common natural disasters) helps for an easy creation of conspiracy stories. The most abject in these stories is the fact that the USA is *demonized* for wanting secretly to destroy parts of mankind in demonic ways (with spreading incurable diseases caused by the artificially created viruses in their laboratories; with radiation that cannot be measured with Geiger's counters, with causing floods, earthquakes or climate changes etc.).

2.2.1 Deprecation of the USA scientific successes

The frustrations toward the USA superiority in the science have no limits. Sometimes they get to a point where well-known successes of the USA, that humanity should be proud of, are negated or deprecated. The most drastic example is probably the Moon landing in 1969 and taking the first steps on the Moon. There are still some individuals who negate this superior achievement whenever possible. There are even "shows" on TV, written texts etc., all in order to negate the Moon landing. There is no doubt that all of this is just another case of anti-USA propaganda. Strong indication for this is the fact that there has never been a serious attempt of negation or deprecation of the Russian space programs for example. I have never met anyone claiming that the first flight into outer space by Yuri Gagarin, as well as other Russian (Soviet) successful space expeditions "never happened". It is the same for the Moon. It is known that in September 1959, the Russians (USSR) were the first to launch a vehicle to land on the Moon. It was the Soviet rocket Luna 2. Have you ever met anyone negating this Soviet (Russian) scientific success? Have you ever heard or read that the Russian Moon landing "did not happen" or that it was a "hoax"? Not only that. Countries as Japan, Great Britain, India, France, China, Israel and others, have also sent their vehicles into space. Have you ever heard or read that their launchings were also "faked" i.e. "filmed in a movie studio"? It is quite the opposite. Every success in the space exploration field is supported and greeted by most people from the world, no matter which country did it. But when it comes to the Americans, they all "lie" about the Moon landing or "have filmed it in a movie studio", etc. I wonder what would the case be if the Russians managed to be the first to send people on Moon; would such hysteria and negation of this scientific achievement exist? The answer of this question can easily be presumed.

But, let's answer this anti-USA provocation. Many people come up with all kinds of conspiracies to disapprove the Moon landing (no need to list them here since they are now irrelevant). These provocateurs (some of which were Americans), realizing that it is not easy to prove the opposite, began to spread their claims that the Moon landing was faked. But recently, all these conspiracy theories were dashed as a bubble of soap. Thanks to the advancements in science, the laser-telescopic system can bounce laser beams off three retro reflector arrays left on the Moon by Apollo 11, 14 and 15, verifying deployment of the Lunar Laser Ranging Experiment at historically documented Apollo Moon landing sites and proving equipment constructed on Earth was successfully transported to the surface of the Moon. In August 2009, NASA's Lunar Reconnaissance Orbiter sent high resolution photos of the Apollo landing sites. These photos show the large Descent Stages of the lunar vehicles, as well tracks of the astronauts' walking paths in the lunar dust.

More proofs will appear for sure as time passes and they will be easily accessible to many people, so I guarantee that this anti-American provocation about the faking of the Moon landing will soon go away in the past as another unsuccessful attempt of negating the USA scientific successes.

In fact, this case clearly shows the evilness of the anti-American provocateurs. They start an anti-American provocation (usually when they think that it is hard to prove the opposite), but when they are defeated with arguments, instead of apologizing and forfeiting – they simply "forget" about their provocation and never talk about it again as if it never existed, till the moment of creating a new one.

2.2.2. Scientific contributions of the USA in benefit of humanity

If there weren't for the Americans, a lot of things we know in today's science would have been unknown. This applies to: astronomy, zoology, botany, physics, chemistry, paleontology, genetics, electronics, medicine, etc. Few are those who approve these contributions to Americans. Others blindly follow only the cases where the bond between the US and science is connected with fabricated evidence or used in a negative context.

The USA today is the leading power in almost every scientific area. American scientists have won 67 Nobel prizes in chemistry, 88 Nobel prizes in physics and 98 Nobel prizes in medicine. Millions of lives throughout the world are being saved thanks to these American discoveries.

From the field of astronomy, we will say that an American created the Hubble space telescope which is the first telescope to show images from other galaxies outside the Milky Way. American scientists have also discovered the Mars moons (Deimos and Phobos), the planet Pluto (that recently lost the status "planet" as it was proven otherwise by an American scientist), cosmic radio-waves, Elliptical galaxies, Neptune satellites, Jupiter, Saturn and Uranus, Cosmic microwave background radiation, rings of Uranus, rings of Jupiter, comets and other heavenly bodies. The Americans have realized a dozen space flights for scientific goals.

The Americans have contributed in chemistry too. Their inventions are the Propane gas, Covalent bonding, Vitamin A, Deuterium, Heavy water, Polyvinylidenechoride, Vitamin E, Sodium Pentothal, Niacin, Antineutron, Cyanoacrylates (super glue), as well as the chemical elements Plutonium, Curium, Americium, Promethium, Berkelium, Californium, Einsteinium, Mendelevium and Seaborgium.

The USA is also the leading country in medicine. Some of their inventions are: Heparin, Smoking-cancer link, a system Homeostasis, antibiotics Streptomycin and Tetracycline, Warfarin (for preventing thrombosis), Polio vaccine, Artificial heart, Artificial neurons, Artificial cardiac pacemaker, Aspartame (for making anti-ulcer drug), Hepatitis B virus vaccine, An Oncogene (a gene that helps turn a normal cell into a tumor cell), Pneumococcal polysaccharide vaccine (for prevent Streptococcus pneumoniae infections such as pneumonia and septicaemia), a tumor suppressor gene, or anti-oncogene (a gene that protects a cell from one step on the path to cancer), embryonic stem cell lines that could one day lead to major medical advancements in organ transplantation as well asgene therapy and treatment of maladies such as paralysis, diabetes, cancer, AIDS and others.

Today in the USA, huge amounts of money from the US taxpayers are used in the field of medicine in order to discover new instruments or ways of improving the human life for the sake of all humanity.

The USA is the leading country in paleontology and paleoanthropology too. In 1974, an American paleoanthropologist discovered the oldest known hominid named Lucy, whose age is estimated to be 3,2 million years. This is considered the greatest discovery in the science that deals with origin of humans. The American paleontologists were also the first to discover the skeletons of a few dinosaurs from tens of millions years ago.

Besides him, American paleontologists were the first to discover skeletons from Hadrosaurus, Torosaurus, Thescelosaurus, Oviraptor and others. These researches still continue nowadays in various parts of the world, mainly with expensive scientific expeditions financed by the American taxpayer's money.

The origins of genetics are also from the USA dating since before the World War two. The Americans discovered the DNA structure and nowadays are leaders in genetics. The USA is spending hundreds of millions of dollars on scientific researches that benefit the whole world. The largest nonprofit scientific and educational institution in the world today is "The National Geographic Society"(NGS), headquartered in Washington, DC. Its interests include geography, archaeology and natural science, the promotion of environmental and historical conversation and the study of world culture and history.

Americans have created many other things that are massively used today. Such are: acrylic paint, airplane, autopilot, computer programs, barcode, BASIC (computer language), electric guitar, bifocal eyeglasses, biological pacemaker, bionic contact lens, bubble gum, bulldozer, cable television, calculator, candy apple, carbonless copy paper, cardiopulmonary bypass - a technique that temporarily takes over the function of the heart and lungs during surgery, cash register, acatalytic converter, chemical laser used in industry for cutting and drilling, clothes hanger, Coca-cola, Comodore 64, communications satellite, cordless telephone, credit card, digital camera, dishwasher, DNA computing, Dolby digital, DOS (operative system), electric microphone, electric stove, electric blanket, electromagnetic lock, electronic paper, e-mail, escalator, fax, fiberglass, first video game, flashlight, floppy disk (with its variants), Frisbee, fuel dispenser, full body scanner, fuses, router, gamma camera, garage door, gas mask, Global Positioning System (GPS), Graphophone, hair spray, Hammond organ, hard-disk drive, highway Hi-Fi, hydraulic brake, IBM RAD 6000 computer, industrial robot, instant camera (Polaroid), internet, ion laser, java script, jeans, jet injector, jukebox, kart racing, computer, keyboard, kinematoscope, laser diode, laser printing, laptop, LCD projector, liquid-crystal display, marker pen, magnetic resonance imaging, micro electromechanical system oscillator, microprocessor, microwave oven, microwave popcorn, mixer (cooking), modem, Monopoly (game), moog synthesizer, mouse (computing), nylon, oil well, operating system, optical mouse, Panavision, paper clip, parking meter, personal computer, photocopier, plasma display, polygraph, popcorn maker, positron emission tomography, quantum cascade laser, radar altimeter, radio telescope, radio carbon dating, random-access memory, refrigerator, relay, remote control, revolving door, Richter magnitude scale, safety pin, safety razor, satellite navigation, sewing machine, Sholes and Glidden typewriter, silica gel, slot machine, solar cell, space observatory, space shuttle, space tourism, spinner (wheel), stereo-pack, supercomputer, supermarket, swivel chair, tablet computer, telephone, tele-printer, television, teleprompter, total internal reflection fluorescence microscope, touch screen, transcriptor, transistor, USB, Ultrabook, universal product code, vacuum cleaner, vacuum tube, vehicle audio, home video game console, videotape, virtual reality, voicemail, vulcanization, washing machine, wearable computer, xerography, workstation, wheel clamp, windscreen wiper, wireless keyboard, wireless LAN zip (file format), zipper and many others.

Even the most pathological Americanophobes use some of these inventions every day, but obviously they do not seem to mind.

The huge participation of the Americans in the movie and the music industry (as well in other art industries) is very well-known and no further explanation is needed.

2.3. Personal and group factors connected with anti-American propagandists

These factors for running the anti-USA propaganda are connected with the propagandists themselves (striking their personal or group ideological or material benefit, their personal frustrations, jealousy, envy etc.).

We will use the ideological aspect as an example. The followers of some ideologies often blame the Americans for their own practical failures or mistakes. For example, the remainders of the communist ideology say that the Americans "destroyed socialism"; Islamic extremists say that the Americans want to "destroy Islam" and lead a "crusade"; Several Balkan and other European nationalists say that the Americans wanted to "destroy" their nation etc.

The anti-USA propaganda on "destroying socialism" (as officially was named the "communism" in the communist countries) contains the following elements:

- Overstressing the positive sides of socialism (satisfactory social security, free education and healthcare, lower crime levels etc.).

- Not mentioning the negative sides of this system (economic collapse, restrictions in electric power and water supply, lack of basic household products:

coffee, olive oil, gasoline..., lack of quality consumer goods, no democracy, totalitarianism, concentration camps, arresting people just because they said something against the government and many others).

- Overstressing the negative sides of capitalism (job layoffs without explanation, increased crime levels and others).

- Not mentioning and marginalizing the positive sides of capitalism (free market, private initiative and a big number of consumer goods, democracy, freedom of speech etc.).

- Not mentioning the mistakes and missteps of the communists as the main reason for the fall of "socialism", but instead blaming the "West", especially the USA, because of their paranoid theory which is the only theory they know.

In fact, I think there is no need to explain the opinions of tens of millions of people who lived in communist regimes in Eastern Europe and other parts of the world. If they enjoyed those regimes so much, these citizens would have massively voted for the communist political parties in their countries in order to "reinstall" these regimes, but they don't even think about such thing and the former communist parties who forcedly ruled in the totalitarian regimes lead by the USSR, barely exist nowadays and have a minor role.

Later we will give an explanation to the reasons of the fall of communist regimes, but first I will say something off topic about the relationship between Russia and the USA. I will explain some things as the way I see them. For decades, the biggest enemy of the USA and of the whole free world was without doubt the danger of communism incarnated in the USSR and other communist countries in the Eastern military bloc. Practically, it was a threat to the physically existence of the western democracies and this period was known as "Cold war" which lasted for over four decades. In that period, we can all agree, that the USA was ready to give countless of millions of dollars to the one who will manage to defeat their biggest enemy – the communist countries, and to deter the threat from communism. But back then the communist countries (mainly the USSR as a nuclear superpower) seemed undefeatable with their large arsenal of nuclear and conventional weaponry, large armies etc. Therefore, the communist bloc and the USSR were nightmares to the USA and other free countries. But suddenly, a miracle happened; the communist bloc and communist regimes collapsed as a tower of cards, starting from 1989 till 1991. Even the strongest optimists did not believe what happened. The nightmare of the USA and other free countries existing for decades had disappeared as a bubble of soap. The communist monster that the USA was ready to give enormous amounts for its defeat was suddenly destroyed. Logically, the USA was supposed to reward the subject who destroyed their biggest enemy and continue to cooperate with it. But who was this subject that destroyed the communist bloc lead by the USSR's evil empire? This subject was not something abstract, in fact it had a name, and that was – the Russian democratic public! The Russian democrats were the decisive factor that destroyed communism and the USSR. Of course, democratic publicities from other countries also took part but decisive was the role of the Russian democrats, supported by millions of Russians. But, what happened next? Logically, the USA was supposed to jump of happiness because someone destroyed their nightmare and they should have thanked the factor that destroyed communism. But the USA administrations seemed unready for what happened next, so several subjects (probably for personal benefits) did not accept the outreach of Russian democrats and did not put the necessary attention, but continued to act as if the "Cold War" was still on. This lead to a disappointment by the Russian democratic publicity, and few years later, the hardcore anti-USA imbued subjects again started to raise voice in Russia and they still have a significant role in the present day's anti-American propaganda. Even though it is not easy, the USA must show real confidence and give support to the democratic forces in Russia. To be partnered with the democratic Russia is of interest to the whole world, including the USA (same as they are partnered with France, Italy, Poland, and other countries).

Now let's get back to the previous topic. I will mention something about Islam. Many Islamic authors claim that the USA wants to "destroy Islam". They overstress the clashes of the USA with some Islamic extremists, but forget to mention the large number of mosques located on the USA territory, unlike the number of churches in some Islamic countries. For example, the USA had 2.106 active mosques in 2011 in which over 2 million and six hundred thousand Muslims could pray freely. Some mosques are event built on the American airports so the Islamic believers could practice their prayers and rituals. Islam is the third largest religion in the USA and today Muslims in the USA have religious freedom and civil rights. There are even Muslim soldiers in the USA army. As of May 2005, the USA army had employed over 15,000 Muslims (*„Muslims in the military: Crescents among the crosses at Arlington Cemetery" alt muslim.* Retrieved 2011-12-06). There are congressmen, ambassadors, mayors and other kind of politicians who are Muslims and there are also two large museums of Islamic culture in the USA. There are American businessmen, actors, writers, musicians, sportsmen, and scientists etc. with Islamic creed who live in the USA and enjoy their freedom and material wealth. All these examples show the wide openness of the USA towards their loyal citizens with Islamic creed. So, there is no basis to claim that the USA is against Islam as a religion.

The USA is against the Islamic terrorism, just as they are against any kind of terrorism no matter the reasons. Simply said, if by "terrorism" we mean murders or attacks on innocent people, then (no matter the reasons why these actions are done) these executers are an impact of the law of any normal country.

A terrorist is someone killing innocent people "in the name of Allah", but also someone killing "in the name of Jesus". In fact, there have been examples of Christian terrorism in the USA (as well as other countries) and the US administration acted the same way as they do with the Islamic terrorists.

For example, in March 10th 1993 the Christian extremist Michael Frederick Griffin murdered Dr. David Gunn in Pensacola, Florida. The reason was that Dr. David Gunn performed abortions in his clinic. Griffin was a member of an extreme Christian sect and killed Dr. Gunn out of his extremist position. Next year in March, Griffin was sentenced to life imprisonment and he is still serving his time. In 2005 his "spiritual guide" John Burt, was sentenced on 18years in prison. Burt was the leader of the extremist Christian sect that terrorized clinics that performed abortions and he died in prison in 2013.

In July 1994 in Florida, the Christian extremist Paul Jennings Hill killed Dr. John Britton and his bodyguard, and wounds his spouse. The reason for this double kill is again abortion. Hill opposed abortions, performed by Dr. Britton, for religious reasons. For these murders Hill was sentenced to death and executed.

In December 1994, the Christian extremist John Salvi (who claimed that he personally knew Jesus) killed two assistants in a clinic in Brookline (Massachusetts) where abortions were performed. He was sentenced to prison where he committed a suicide in 1996.

In 1993, the Christian extremist Shelley Shannon wounded both hands of Dr. George Tiller because he performed abortions in his clinic. She was sentenced to

11 years in prison.

There have been other murders or acts of violence by individual Christian extremists or small groups and they were all treated according the law. Many activists of the extreme Christian sect "Army of God" were arrested and sentenced mainly because of attacking doctors and clinics that performed abortions.

Let's say a word regarding the nationalists who claimed that "the USA wants to destroy their nation and country". Here we can see some tragic yet comic situations. For example, Serbian nationalists say that the USA wanted to "destroy Serbia and Serbian people", but this exact same thing is said by some Macedonian, Greek, Bulgarian, Bosnian, Croatian and other nationalists, besides the oppositeness of their individual nationalisms although these nationalisms often are opposed to each other.

There are marginal individuals or small groups of Macedonian nationalists in my country Republic of Macedonia who claim that "the USA wants to destroy Macedonia" (even though the USA has always been friendly with Macedonia and President Roosevelt pledged for creating an independent Macedonian state in times where Macedonia was divided between other countries). Most of these "nationalists" are former communists and it is a fact that they spread anti-USA propaganda, claiming that the USA gave support to Greece with an aim to "destroy Macedonia". On the other hand, Greek nationalists claim the opposite – the USA is supporting Macedonia and is "secretly working against Greece and Greek people". Greek nationalists have even organized large anti-USA demonstrations in Thessaloniki in 2004. Some Greek intellectuals, even some former ministers, continue to write publicly that the USA wanted to "destroy Greece and Greek people". As one of the many examples, we will draw attention to a part of an analysis named "Who wants to destroy Greece?" made by a famous Greek composer and foreign minister named Mikis Theodorakis published on 5.5.2010 in the "Volitaire Network" edition (Athens http://www.voltairenet.org/article 165350.html). In his statement, Mikis Theodorakis is without doubt blaming the USA for the economic crisis in Greece, claiming that the USA wanted to destroy Greece and the Greek people. In his text, besides the reasons for the economic crisis in Greece, we also read:

I have therefore come to the conclusion that there are some people who made us feel guilty and alarmed us for the purpose of steering us towards the IMF, which is a pillar of US expansionist policy, and all the talk about European solidarity is only a subterfuge to hide that the whole thing is purely a US initiative to sink us into an artificial economic crisis so that our people will be scared, will buckle under, will give up their precious possessions and will finally kneel down and accept foreign domination. But why? To serve which plans and objectives?

Virtually all the countries surrounding us have hopped on the US bandwagon. We are the odd ones out, taking the blows without even realizing it, from the time of the Military Junta dictatorship and the 40% loss of Cyprus, to the mortifying controversy with Skopje (Former Yugoslav Republic of Macedonia) and the ultra-nationalist Albanians.

There is a design to destroy us as a people, which is exactly what is happening today.

So we have Macedonian nationalists who claim that the USA wanted to destroy Macedonia in favor of Greece and we have Greek nationalists (even moderate politicians like Theodorakis) who claim that the USA wanted to destroy Greece in favor of Macedonia. Isn't this funny, considering that Macedonian and Greek nationalists can't stand each other? A logical question appears: how is it possible for the Americans to "destroy" both Greeks and Macedonians at the same time? This is the level of absurdity the paranoid Americanophobia can get.

There are many examples as these. If you just check the programs of the nationalists and chauvinistic political parties and other kinds of organizations from different countries and regions of the world, you can see that most of these programs are anti-USA and many have attitudes and articulations that the USA is acting towards "destroying" their country and nation. What is hypocritical here is that these statements are made by parties and organizations that (if they had the power) would have destroyed other nations and countries in benefit of their country. In any case, it is a good thing that most of the national-chauvinistic people from various countries (who have caused many wars or other kinds of disasters) are afraid of the USA.

While we are on the conspiracy theories on "destroying" smaller nations and countries by the USA as those propagated by the nationalists, it is not clear why the USA would "conspire" about destroying a smaller country? Simply, if the USA decides to get rid of a country, their level of power is allowing them to do that openly! There is no need for conspiracies.

We will also mention the accusations on racism in the USA, in a period where Barack Obama who descends from an Afro-American family was chosen for his second term as US president by a majority of Caucasian Americans. As a reminder, African-Americans are only around 12% of the USA population, but they have a President of the country for two terms. We will not mention other famous Afro-Americans in the USA from the fields of politics, sport, art... because they are widely known, but we will ask a question: Can a man with African descent be elected as a president of the state or government in some European country? According to the statistics, around 10% of the population in France is of

Arab origin, around 3.5% are of African origin and 1.5% is of Oriental-Asian origin. Will one of them ever become President or Prime minister of France? Around 15% of the population is of Oriental-Asian origin in Russia. Can one of them (maybe a Chechen or a Tatar) hope for a Presidential or Prime Minister position in Russia? Not only that. Name how many countries have a member of ethnical or racial minority freely elected as a leader by the majority in free and democratic elections, in a country where his ethnical or racial group is a minority? Can anyone imagine a member of the Arabian minority in Israel becoming President of Israel, or the president of Serbia being a member of the Albanian, Hungarian or gypsy minority? This applies to almost every country. Few are those who blame other countries for racism unlike the USA, even though their President is African-American. This is just another proof of the frustration of the anti-USA propagandists.

I am not saying that there are no problems with racism in the USA. I want to point out that those problems appear in other countries too, but only the problems in the USA are widely presented and judged by the media, although the USA is the only country in the world in which the Caucasian majority elected an African-American as their President.

We will also say something about the absurdity of labeling the American tourists as "spies" as some individuals from small and poor countries do. In wealthier countries, maybe there are reasons for sending "spies", but what would this large number of "American spies" do in a small and poor country? Who and what would they "spy"?

In context of this subtitle, I will also mention the ordinary jealousy towards the USA's power as a reason for anti-USA propaganda. This reason is registered in some subjects from the Western European countries too. Maybe this is the best time to tell an anecdote:

An Englishman talked with an American and sarcastically said: "What kind of nation are you Americans? You don't even know your grandfathers and grand grandfathers" (implying that the USA is a relatively new nation compared to the European countries). The American answered this cynical notice with a simple answer: "We may not know who are grandfathers are, but we damn sure know who their grandchildren are."

The point is clear. Many European countries are centuries older than the USA, but today they are less powerful than USA and they can't do anything else but to tell stories about their "glorious past".

Speaking of jealousy, this is without doubt one of the main emotional reasons for some individuals to hate the USA. It is common for the frustrated and insufficiently realized persons to hate the successful and the unmatchable, so they empty their negative energy by hating the successful. They do this because of the insufficient self-realization and their personal failures in their private lives. A very similar story can be found in a fable by Aesop in which the fox, unable to reach the delicious ripe grape, starts to attack it because supposedly it was "distasteful and unready". It is the same case with a big part of the Americanophobes. If some of them try to present their pathological Americanophobia as a "fight for human rights", then a simple question appears: Why don't they also fight for human rights against the administrations of other countries, where these rights are more vulnerable?

Especially pathetic are those Americanophobes who have never visited the USA and have no idea what kind of state it is, but hate this country just because someone else told them to do that.

There are Americanophobes who have been to the USA, even lived there, but after returning to their countries they start to spread and nurture hatred. It is clear that these kinds of Americanophobes hate the USA just because some of their personal ambitions were not fulfilled while staying there, so the animosity and hatred towards the factors that interfered with their ambitions slowly transformed into hatred for the USA and Americans.

The anti-USA propagandists do not care which political option is governing the USA: republicans or democrats. Most of the Americanophobes do not even know these parties exist in the USA. The only enemies they have are the "Americans" (regardless of who governs them).

3. PSYCHOLOGICAL BACKGROUND AS A REASON FOR ACCEPTING THE ANTI-AMERICAN PROPAGANDA IN THE POST-COMMUNIST COUNTRIES

To explain the psychological background as a reason for accepting the articulations of the anti-USA propaganda by part of publicity from the post-communist countries, we ought to give some additional explanations that are barely known by the Western publicity, because they did not live in communist regimes. The West knows some theoretical information about these regimes, but they lack practical experience – the experience from being in jail is not the same with the experience gained from reading about how is it to be in jail.

The communist regimes were totalitarian. We will not focus on all their segments (besides negative, there have been positive too), but mostly on the topic we deal with. The information in this system was strictly controlled. The relatively lower level of scientific achievements in the fields of technique compared to today also contributed in this. Back then, there was no internet on which anyone can freely find information; there were no satellite programs that freely broadcasted TV channels from all over the world. Back then, the people were mainly informed by several strictly controlled government newspapers, by one or two TV channels and a few radio stations that were all censored and under strict state control. Some individuals listened to foreign radio stations at times, but it was strictly prohibited and those individuals risked going in jail.

Furthermore, most property in communism was "social" (literally translated - everyone's, but practically – no one's, i.e. the property in fact belonged to the state). The kind of "everyone's and no one's" (but in fact, state) property created irresponsibility at workplaces. Salaries were guaranteed by the state, so whether someone will work or not, he will still get his salary at the end of each month. Many workers started to skive at work, aware that whether they will work or "rest" at work they will still get the same salary as everyone. The enterprises were state owned, so hardly anyone cared for the work discipline (unlike the private enterprises, where owners care about how much their workers work).

The nature of the ownership of the workplaces in communism (or as the communists say – "socialism") was probably the most important reason for this system's collapse. Simply, no one had motive to work in the state companies, unlike the private companies where the main motive for work is profit. I think there is no need of further explanations for understanding this simple truth.

In practice, there has been no serious private initiative for economy in the communist regimes. Almost the entire economy was under state control. This proved as disastrous in daily lives of citizens. For example, whenever a lack of a certain everyday product appeared, it was up to the massive bureaucratic state machines to organize an import of that product, instead of allowing the private mobile importers to immediately bring that product on the market.

So, the leading communists realized that the economy is going to collapse. The people, on one way or another, began to demand accountability for the poor economic situation. The communists faced a dilemma. They either had to admit their own mistakes and risk losing their power or had to point a serious culprit for the bad situation they created. But admitting their own mistakes never even occurred in their minds since that would have led to question the fundament of their existence – the political system and the ideology they have spread and above all, the danger of losing authority. On the other hand, they had to point out a "culprit" for the bad situation in order to "calm down" the people. So, they created an "external enemy" as the "main culprit" responsible for all the evilness in their state. In fact, this story is common for all the totalitarian and non-democratic regimes. The communists were not guilty according to the communist propaganda, because if they admitted the truth, they would have been lynched by the citizens. That is why a fabricated "external enemy" was "responsible" (a commonly used stigma in the rhetoric back then). The people were given a culprit to whom they could direct and empty their negative energy and dissatisfaction of the bad life. These villains of the piece i.e. the "external enemies" were usually the CIA and the Americans, the Vatican, Islam and others. The communists fabricated different "external enemies" suitable for everyone's taste, and the citizens were brainwashed by this propaganda since it was a time with lack of free media. This caused many people today to have consequences in the way of thinking. They don't blame themselves for all state, collective or personal failures, but they constantly search for an external factor to blame. Simply, this code is deeply rooted in their conscious and subconscious. All their lives they are taught to think this way and they can't think otherwise. Since a young age, they have a built-in paranoia against everything that is coming from outside. This pathological animosity is probably one of the roughest consequences from the communist propaganda machine.

Thus, these people are easily subjected to the anti-USA propaganda. What is interesting is that many of them try to transfer this point of view to their children, even though younger generations live in a time of democracy, internet and cable television so this paranoid and one-sided reasoning barely has a base.

3.1. The artistic freedom in the USA as a reason for an anti-USA propaganda

We will mention another paradoxical moment in this topic, and that is the high level of artistic freedom in the USA as a reason for anti-USA propaganda. To explain this, we will use one characteristic example. We will again mention the American Vietnamese war. Up to this day, around 80 movies have been filmed in the USA on this topic. Besides them, there are tens of episodes from TV shows in which this war is mentioned and there are also a certain number of documentary movies. In a significant part of these movies, besides the positive role of the American army, there are also scenes where American soldiers kill innocent Vietnamese civilians. Of course if some authors of American movies based on the Vietnam War include such kinds of scenes, they do this because of the high level of freedom that USA has. But how are these scenes received by the other countries in the world? Here a paradoxical situation happens. Namely, few are those who react with praising the artistic freedom in the USA, i.e. few are those who say "I admire the level of freedom in the USA where you can freely film scenes in which Americans are presented in a negative context". Instead, many comment on these scenes with: "This is a proof of how evil the Americans were in Vietnam. You can see this even in their movies". Why is it like this? Simply because it is unimaginable in many countries to film movies in which the "dirty side" of their own history is presented. I am not saying that there are administrative bans on this (even though they exist in some countries), but it is more of an untold "consensus", i.e. some kind of generally accepted self-censorship on not touching these topics. We already mentioned that France waged war with Vietnam for over eight decades. Do you know how many French movies are based on the

French Vietnamese War? The answer is – only one fully filmed in a French production and two other filmed in a co-production! It is a taboo-topic for the French people, so even though they fought way longer against the Vietnamese, we barely know nowadays what really happened in the French-Vietnamese war. It is clear that this way France wants to protect their national interest, by trying to put their 8 decade war on Vietnam in oblivion. In addition, there is no administrative ban in France initiated by the government or other subjects on filming these kinds of movies – simply said, it is like this topic is affected by a general consensus.

Even more drastic is the example with other countries. Even though the artistic freedom is guaranteed by the law in many countries, if someone films such movie in a rare occasion, he will be labeled as a "betrayer" with the possibility of encountering unpleasantness. It is a different case in the USA. There you can film movies on criticizing the present or past official American policies and they can receive high honors and awards. Hence, this puts the USA in another paradox. Their expression on freedom instead of being an incitement for other countries to free their art to the level of creating works with context against their actual national interest, it became an incitement of hatred against the USA as a "non-democratic country" that "makes war with foreign territories and nations".

It is the same case with American movies on other negative events from the USA past such as: the conflict with Native Americans, criminal competition between gangs in the first half of 20th century, movies dedicated to mass murderers etc. Simply, the level of consciousness of the people (especially those in the post-totalitarian regimes) is such that they would rather accuse the USA based on what they see in American movies, than honor them for the high level of artistic freedom that USA has.

4. MEANS AND WAYS OF LEADING
THE ANTI-AMERICAN PROPAGANDA

As any other propaganda, the anti-USA too is led by well-known appropriate means and ways. They often are:

Media, printed or electronic; it is known that television is dominant in the informative sphere. Most relevant issues in the topic we are writing about are: TV news and TV debates.

TV news. I have noticed that the TV news from one private national TV station from my country (which was later closed for unpaid debts and the owner put in jail due to tax evasion), whenever a specific editor regulated them, have almost always started with an information about the USA in a negative connotation. This information included a wide range of events: a local killing, a robbery, car accident, as well statements against the USA policy made by more or less significant politicians etc. Other TV stations also act this way. If some day goes without "spectacular" negative events from which news against the USA would have been created, they would search the internet for all kinds of statistical information connected with the USA and again form information about the USA in a negative connotation such as the number of people who died from smoking in the USA, the increased percent of school violence in the USA, the increased poverty etc. Hence, they do not even mention these kinds of problems in other countries. Their goal is to show the USA in a bad light at all costs.

TV Debates. During the time of communism, a lonely monk named Gavril lived in a monastery in Macedonia. He was a very intelligent man with a PhD and he also was a sculptor. During one of my visits to this monastery, he said to me something that I still remember and quote it in appropriate situations. We were talking about how religion is represented on television (which was strictly controlled by the atheist-communist regime at that time) and the friar Gavril said (paraphrasing):

"Communists are weird. When they want to make a TV debate on economy, they call economists. When they want to make a debate on sport, they call sportsmen or sports professionals. It is the same with art, health or any other topic. In all the debates dedicated on these topics, appropriate experts on those fields are invited. But, when they want to make a debate on religion, they call interlocutors that are exclusively – atheists"

This was the truth. Only those who negate it and the enemies (atheists) could talk about religion on TV, because in the communism, atheism was imposed as a part of the state ideology. I have mentioned this event with the monk because the same "story" happens nowadays with the anti-USA propaganda. So far, I have watched a few Balkan TV stations with TV debates devoted on the US foreign policy and no American or any kind of supporter of that policy was ever invited. Those who were invited to talk were always established opponents and enemies of the US foreign policy (former communist activists or communist scouts, several anti-American "analysts," etc.) Extreme tendencies are the main features of these "debate" TV programs that also have an impact on the viewers.

Radio. The ways and forms through which the television operates are the same with the radio and the printed media, but the printed media is most suitable for reacting with denials and running polemics with the anti-USA propagandists.

Books. The books with anti-USA content are using the same methods that we have mentioned so far, and those are simplicity and lack of impartiality when representing the arguments in order to demonize the

75

USA.

Printed media. A large number of countries have newspapers in which almost every edition has a text with an anti-American content. These newspapers have Americanophobes on duty who throws poisonous arrows against everything American (politics, culture, history...). What is very underhanded in these newspapers is that in some of them, their editors (or owners) disallow publishing denials of their anti-American pamphlets (for which I have personal experience with a daily newspaper from my country, known as a den of anti-American propaganda).

Internet. In the last few years, one of the most important mediums used for spreading the anti-USA propaganda is without doubt the internet. Websites, blogs, profiles or groups on social networks are created and they post information with anti-American content. Some of the owners of these are anonymous, which can be an indication that they are created by intelligence services of countries that are not in a good relationship with the USA. As one of the numerous examples of this, we will mention the website http://worldnewsdailyreport.com which fabricates insolent lies in order to denigrate the USA in front of the world. Every text from this website is intelligently created nonsense decorated with data, pictures etc. in order to look more convincing to the naive. Because of the fact that it can be easily determined that texts from this website are pure fiction with just a simple search, and because of the fact that the identity of the sick minds that are behind this website is unknown, it becomes clear that a foreign service is behind it. In the meantime, it is sad that some serious websites and portals all over the world share contents from this burrow of the anti-USA propaganda (as it was the recent fabricated "testimony" by the supposed "former CIA agent, who claims that he killed Marilyn Monroe" and similar nonsense).

Public debates. The anti-USA propagandists use every of their public appearances to throw a "poisonous arrow" against the USA. Even when, for example, they talk about medicine, history, sport, agriculture, literature, or when they promote someone's book – they always find a place in their speech to introduce an inappropriate remark against the USA.

Personal conversations. There are anti-American propagandists, who literally walk from man to man and open conversations in which they accuse the USA of being the source of all evilness in the world. Their impact is insignificant, but still worth to be registered.

5. WAYS OF OPPOSING THE ANTI-USA PROPAGANDA

So far we have seen that the anti-American propaganda with its comprehensiveness and aggressiveness is a serious threat to the USA's reputation and the Americans as a people. Because of that, an organized and efficient opposition is needed. Not only the American factors, but the numerous friends the USA has from around the world should also join this process. Only then is a successful defeat of the anti-American propaganda possible.

Some of the measures that should be taken are the following:

1. Forming friendship associations amongst the indigenous people in the states where it is possible, especially in those with more aggressive anti-USA propaganda. This way, at least part of the USA's friends will be mobilized. These domicile associations, apart from the positive activities, should also have an obligatory informational activity. Simply, for every groundless anti-American provocation published in a medium, they should react with a counter-information in the same or another medium. Thus, they should mark

the individual journalists, editors, analytics, redactions and other subjects who constantly and tendentiously spread untruths and lies against the USA and they should be publically labeled as "anti-American propagandists". That way, they will be "marked" by the public and all their future articulations will be devalued in advance, i.e. the public will be ready for their articulations. Namely, whenever someone reads or hears an anti-American propagandistic articulation, he will know that the author (or medium) of it is not objective because he is an established "anti-American propagandist". An unscrupulous media war is needed at every place and everywhere, unlike the present situation in some Balkan countries and beyond, where elements of the anti-USA propaganda are "on stage" with hardly anyone opposing them. Anti-American propagandists do not have many proofs for their articulations, so many of them avoid getting into polemics after adducing their arguments (for which I have a lot of personal experiences of my so-far polemics against some of the anti-American propagandists from Macedonia or foreigners). Usually, after the first denials I indicate on their writings, they cowardly withdraw from polemics. For example, what would an anti-American propagandist answer when I ask him why do they persistently talk about the American Vietnamese war only, and not about the French one which was 10 times longer? Of course that question has no rational answer, but the problem is that someone **has to ask** these questions! So, friends of the USA should be asked to follow everything that the media from their countries is talking or writing about the USA, and they should immediately react if they notice any kind of false imputation or tendentious informing. To every article – react with counter-article! To every statement – a counter-statement! It is true that the freedom of information should be respected and nobody calls that into question. But if someone has a democratic right to write, for example, that the USA purposely created the avian influenza, then the one who will respond that his claim is an absolute nonsense and that the carrier of that information is nothing but a frustrated Americanophobe, has also a democratic right to act. If the democratic right is not used in these provocations, I will say it again, part of the public will get the impression that those imputations are true. Sometimes even the USA's ambassadors should send denials to certain lies that are being sold in the countries they work in.

It is necessary to explain why it is very important for the indigenous citizens – friends of the USA - to join the media war against the anti-USA propaganda. It is known that every nation and culture has its own way of internal communication that depends on several factors (mentality, socio-historical circumstances etc.). For example, some nations have a more "dynamic" mentality, so their way of communication is different than (figuratively speaking) the nations with more "calmed" mentality. This is why compatibility in the way of communicating at the respective nation (culture) is needed. Let us illustrate this using a fictitious example (that is not so far from the truth). Let's say a provocateur writes in a daily newspaper from one of the Balkan countries that: "The Americans are the evilest nation in the world because they have invented AIDS and the avian influenza in order to destroy other nations". In the next edition, we see an article saying that the USA embassy of the same country spent a large sum on reconstructing a poor village school. A question appears: Will the school reconstruction leave a higher impression on the neutral readers compared to the rude provocation by the anti-American propagandist, i.e. is the reconstruction of the poor school an adequate answer to the unscrupulous claim that the Americans are creating viruses for destroying nations? The answer is – an explicit no! An average reader would welcome the school reconstruction, but on the other hand he will shudder from the American "monstrous purpose" of "creating viruses" and destroying whole nations (something he read in the same newspaper and probably will think it is "true" since no one refuted it). This is why a same type of answer is needed for the rude anti-American provocation! In the next newspaper edition (or some of the next), it should be responded that the provocateur writing these things have no idea what he is talking about since he can check facts wherever he wants and educate himself that the AIDS virus originated in Africa and the avian influenza in China (the Chinese themselves admitted). The style of responding should be in accordance with **the style (level) of communication** of the indigenous people (culture) from that country. If the provocation is rude and indelicate – the respond should be the same way. This also means that if the provocation is written on a more sophisticated level, the same should be with the respond. Once, an American diplomat responded to the anti-American provocations from one Balkan country with (paraphrasing): "We are slandered in the media, but we will patiently continue to help this country" (alluding that he has no intention of responding to these attacks). This kind of approach is wrong (at least for the Third world countries) since it does not suit the level of communication (mentality) of the largest part of these nations. It is like trying to install a cutting edge digital television in a city where most people have old black-and-white TVs with analog antennas – it would be in vain since they do not have the receivers to watch it. On the opposite, give them analog programs in accordance with their receivers, and the digitalization will come later.

Of course, I do not think that the workers from the USA embassies should respond to all the anti-USA provocations and argue in the media with the anti-Americans, but this is something that should be done by the indigenous friends of the USA who know the mentality of their people (the way of communicating). For now, at least from my humble opinion, the USA's friends from particular states hardly ever engage in the media defense against the anti-American provocateurs, but they expose their friendship with the USA mainly when they have to apply for grants in the USA embassy. This practice should be changed.

2. Publicly expressing respect for the culture and traditions of people from every country. I think that here (at least on the Balkan, even beyond) the USA is acting on a satisfactory level.

3. Providing material aid for the indigenous people, especially in the poorer environments. Two things are important here:

a) The material aid should be as "visible" as possible and should be intended for the needs of general public. For example, it is better for the USA (using their governmental or non-governmental organizations) to build a playground park for public use than to give loans to some indigenous businessmen that will start enterprises from which few will benefit. There is also the danger of abusing the loans, as it previously has happened (it is a known case of the USA giving a large sum of loan to a Macedonian businessman who instead of investing it in his medium, he bought frozen chicken so he could trade. Later on he was called to court by the USA, and in return he started an anti-American pro-paganda using his mediums. This person is in prison today for other financial speculations to the detriment of the Macedonian state).

b) The media in the respective country should be notified for every, including the smallest material aids.

4. Reaching out to the youth. I do not think it would be a huge expense for the USA to finance a tour of the music or film stars in the countries of the Third world where an anti-USA propaganda is led. The youth is

hungry for those kinds of spectacles, but the countries (or their private distributers) are too poor to pay the visits of such stars. This is why these tours should be helped financially (maybe a show for a certain celebration or a holiday). Then, it should be emphasized directly or discreetly (depending on conditions) that these tours are made possible thanks to the USA government or another **American** institution. This way, they youth will *know* that they have met their idols thanks to the USA.

5. Cooperation with the pro-USA oriented intellectuals.

6. Being prudent when financing particular domicile non-governmental organizations. It is not enough for one to say that he stands for "democracy" so that he could receive money from the USA embassy. Lets' explain this. In one country, the political party A is elected for many years in a row now. This party is favored by the people and is also pro-USA oriented. The opposition (political party B) uses hits below the belt to attack the government that is supported by the majority of the people. The opposition formed several alleged "non-governmental" organizations which demanded money from the US embassy for organizing "debates on democracy". The embassy gave them money, believing that those debates will be truly on democracy. However, not one government representative was invited, but only the politicians from the opposition, so these debates were used as a camouflage for slanders and attacks on the government. This way the citizens gain a repellent impression that the US embassy is funding anti-governmental actions, even though the government is uncompromisingly pro-USA and pro-Western oriented and supported by majority of the people. In this way, the embassy is naively deceived by the alleged "democrats" who in fact are just trying to come to power at all costs. Besides that, the government gains an unpleasant feeling that their US friends have inappropriately

financed anti-governmental actions. Unfortunately, there have been a few cases like these and that is a reason why prudence is needed when deciding who and what will be financed by the American institutions i.e. discovering what is the true purpose and goal of those asking for money from the USA embassies (or USAID), falsely representing themselves as "fighters for human rights" with an ultimate goal to come to power.

7. Another key factor for the failure or success of the anti-USA propaganda is of course the USA foreign policy itself, which should be to continue making friends throughout the world, but also keep on providing a resolute response to the extremely violent movements that practice terrorism.

*

Surely there are other ways of dealing with the anti-USA propaganda, which together with the already mentioned, can deal a serious blow to the disclosure of this propaganda.

6. ABOUT THE AUTHOR

Aleksandar DONSKI is born on November 1960 in Shtip, Republic of Macedonia. He originates from an artistic family. He graduated on the faculty of History of Art with archaeology on the University of "St. Cyril and Methodius" in Skopje and has a Masters from the University of "Goce Delchev" in Shtip where he works as an executive of the University library and as a member of the Institute of History and Archaeology. He is an author of 25 books based on history, folklore, religion and literature, as well a few hundred articles in newspapers, magazines and on the internet. He is also an author of a large number of TV and radio documentary programs regarding history, folklore and his travels, for which he has received awards and acknowledgements.

Contact address: adonski@t-home.mk

www.ingramcontent.com/pod-product-compliance
Lightning Source LLC
Chambersburg PA
CBHW070300290526
45791CB00003B/1024